Men of Steel Discipline

The Official Oral History of Black Pioneers in the Martial Arts

Published by:

Modern Bu-jutsu, Inc.
6948 N. Western Ave.
Chicago, IL 60645

Chief Editor: Jennifer Harris Baarman
Editors: Alistair Stewart Couper and Maria Redona Couper
Layout & Design: Benita Couper Rahming
Cover Design: Boecher Studios
Photos: Keith Taylor

ISBN: 0-9627898-9-5
Library of Congress #: 94-78600

MAR 96

KN

Dedication

The learning experience of this historical and literary journey was one of great joy and passion. We feel very fortunate in that we have been afforded the rare opportunity to talk with these distinguished gentlemen.

During the initial stages of researching this text, efforts were made to locate known and unknown black gentlemen contributors to the martial arts. And we wish to thank the many who made this path toward knowledge easier to travel.

This book is dedicated to the many black pioneers of the martial arts, for it is partly through their blood, sweat, and tears that the quality of life of thousands of people have been greatly enhanced.

William F. Hinton ,1994

D'Arcy J. Rahming, 1994

Table of Contents

Louis Moseley (left) and Bill Downs. Photo Courtesy of Louis Moseley

Introduction

Dedication. Sacrifice. Personal challenge. This book includes conversations with 10 men who took time to share their thoughts about their involvement in the martial arts. These men are all black pioneers in the martial arts and have dedicated their lives to practicing and teaching its principles. They have been strong role models for children. They strove to instill a sense of success and drive in their students in the hopes that their students will pass on knowledge of the martial arts, so that each student will have a positive influence on his or her community.

Each of these men have at least thirty years of dedicated training. They learned when the martial arts were at their infancy in the United States. They became leaders and teachers when "Jim Crow" was alive and well, in full practice in the South and in true spirit in the North. All were chosen for this project because of their exposure to many of the world's foremost teachers and their extensive knowledge of black contributions to the martial arts.

During World War II, many black pioneers were called upon to teach hand-to-hand combat skills to American soldiers. After the war, the U.S. occupied Japan. U.S. military personnel, including blacks, who had tours of duty there, had further exposure to the oriental martial arts. Many of these men gained significant knowledge during this period. When they returned home, they continued their training, often in the back of pool halls or basements or wherever they were allowed to establish a class. Blacks were not formally received into many of the martial arts organizations until the late 1950s.

Within this historical context, the accomplishments of these black pioneers are all the more admirable. Many experienced some form of racism and adversity early in their careers, but they overcame these

Men of Steel Discipline

obstacles. They have all made substantial contributions to their local communities as well as the martial art community. Some have been instrumental in organizing study of the ancient roots of black involvement in the martial arts. Some are world renowned as teachers and administrators. Some are not so well known. All played a significant role in the development of the arts in the United States. We invite you to share their wisdom, their vision, and their love of the martial arts.

Sensei Louis Moseley

During the 1960s and 1970s Louis Moseley played a vital role in the growth of Karate in the Midwest. Through the direct efforts of Moseley and other prominent instructors, the United States Karate Association (USKA) became one of the largest American organizations of its time.

Moseley was born May 24, 1926 on Chicago's south side. He began his training in 1939 in the arts of Jujutsu and Judo. In 1954 under the authorization of 8th degree Black Belt Sensei Mas Tamura, Moseley chartered the first martial arts club on Chicago's North Shore at the Emerson YMCA. In 1956 Moseley was introduced to Karate and by 1962 he had received instructor status and was active in promoting Karate.

Moseley withdrew from active teaching in the late 1970s. He leaves a legacy of having paved the way for the participation of other black instructors and students in a national martial arts organization.

I started training in the martial arts in 1939 in Chicago. I don't remember the name of the Dojo [training hall]. It's no longer there. It was in a little house right off of a Buddhist temple in a small Japanese community.

I was thirteen. I was the only American in the school then. I never saw any other Americans there before I left and went to the Ju-jutsu Institute, also in Chicago. I became a student of Masato Vince Tamura. That was around 1940-1941. I studied there until I went into the service in 1944.

From 1944 to 1947 I was stationed primarily in the Philippines. I was the Chief Unarmed Defense Instructor for our Air Force base, the Thirteenth Air Force. I had an opportunity to go to Hoshikowa Air Force Base, where I located a second Ju-jutsu school. As a result of myself and a 5th fleet marine, the Ju-jutsu school set up what they called a foreign section. We came in, basically during all of our time off, when they had special classes.

We had classes during the day and evening. Three evenings a week the master Senseis [instructors], we used to call them the grand masters, would come in and take over the school and work with us. During the day we would work with the main instructors of the school.

I received my first degree black belt in Ju-jutsu in Japan in 1946. After my overseas tour, I returned to this country and began to teach Ju-jutsu at the Ju-jutsu Institute for Prof. Tamura. Subsequently, in 1954 I opened the first martial arts school along the North Shore at the Emerson YMCA in Evanston. At that time, the only other school in the area was a Judo school run by Henry Okamura.

In about 1956 I was introduced to Karate. I saw a demonstration of it at the Ju-jutsu Institute, Sensei Natahe did Shorin Ryu. He came from Japan to visit, to spend some time with Tamura and I joined his class as a white belt. In 1961 I received my black belt in Karate and became an instructor for the United States Karate Association in 1962, I believe, at the Emerson Street YMCA.

I was a program analyst for the United States Navy, Great Lakes Naval Base during the day. I was at the Great Lakes for 30 years. I retired in 1981, as a personnel director for the Naval hospital in Great Lakes. Again, I was kind of tied into working with people and instructing people as the personnel director.

My Karate training was with John Keehan, Master Keoppel, with that group. The training was well organized. It was highly disciplined. The students had a lot of respect for the main Sensei and the instructors appointed by the Senseis to run things. It was like a training institution because the advanced students were given the opportunity to conduct some of the exercise classes, to take small groups and train them in Kata [prearranged fighting forms]. There was never any freestyle fighting.

Louis Moseley Photo Courtesy of Louis Moseley

This was our recognized rule which I tried to implement in my teaching, unless it was controlled to avoid any type of injuries. That was one of the things I remember most.

We had Kata specified by belt ranks. Before you could obtain your first degree black belt, there were designated Kata forms that you had to learn. Different belt levels could only work certain Katas until they were in training for the next level. And then they would have an advanced student teach them. When I was an advanced student I got a lot of experience teaching and improving my own form because I was constantly out there teaching under the supervision of the Sensei.

In 1970 I was also fortunate when the Navy, the federal government itself, came up with a policy to have an exercise program for the military people. And at Great Lakes they voted and they wanted a martial arts program. So the base commanding officer authorized my commanding officer to allow me, since he knew I had certification from the United States Karate Association, to teach on a daily basis and the Great Lakes Martial Arts Club was formed. I taught from 11 a.m. to 1 p.m., Monday through Friday.

Practice was very physical, not abusive-type physical, but basically building up your own endurance. At Great Lakes, say from good weather on, we worked outside. We did a lot of running to the class and running from the class and then we worked outside. We also worked out in the swimming pool to build up the legs. And the classes we had, when I was coming up on my belt rank, were quite physical as far as developing endurance. Karate classes were interesting, but they were highly controlled and highly supervised. The Kata classes were the most interesting to me.

I seem to enjoy personal gain from doing Kata. Fighting is something that lasts a few minutes, whereas I felt I could develop myself more and more working Kata. In the inner strength I learned to breathe and I learned to balance. And I could see

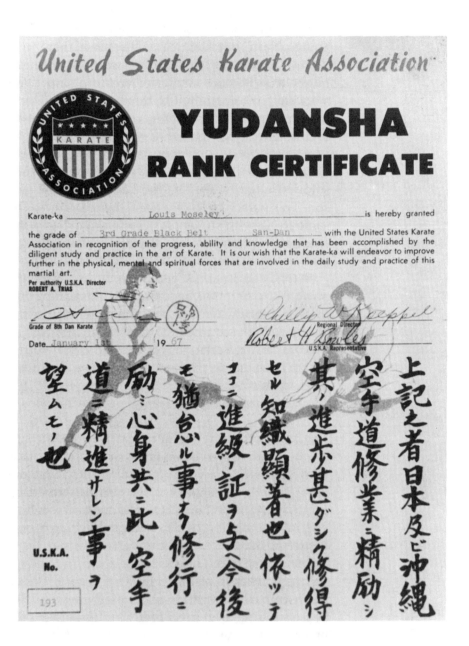

United States Karate Association

YUDANSHA RANK CERTIFICATE

Karate-ka _____ Louis Moseley _____ is hereby granted

the grade of ___ 3rd Grade Black Belt _____ San-Dan _____ with the United States Karate Association in recognition of the progress, ability and knowledge that has been accomplished by the diligent study and practice in the art of Karate. It is our wish that the Karate-ka will endeavor to improve further in the physical, mental and spiritual forces that are involved in the daily study and practice of this martial art.

Per authority U.S.K.A. Director
ROBERT A. TRIAS

Grade of 8th Dan Karate

Date January 1st 19 67

Regional Director

Robert H Bowles
U.S.K.A. Representative

U.S.K.A.
No.

193

上記之者日本及ビ沖縄空手道修業ニ精励シ其ノ進歩甚ダシク修得セル知織顕著也依ッテ進級ノ証ヲ与ヘ今後モ猶怠ル事ナク修行ニ励ミ心身共ニ此ノ空手道ニ精進サレン事ヲ望ムモノ也

Moseley's third degree black belt certificate Courtesy of Louis Moseley

personal growth week by week, day by day, by doing Kata.

My training gave me an opportunity to have more tolerance of other people. As a personnel director, I encountered people with all kinds of problems. Some of the problems I knew were fake, and where, without some martial arts discipline, I might have jumped at the person and said, `You are a liar,' or something like that, I learned to listen. I learned to reason better. I learned to project myself into what the other person was doing or was trying to do and become more objective and then try to deal with it. I tried to find some kind of solution other than to be too harsh with this person. This person probably needs help. I can see the same thing with students. In spite of having many students in the class, I can easily spot the person who needs the most attention, isolate that person, give that person ample attention, but yet not take away from the other people in the class and make them feel they're wasting their time. In my school, I try to develop competent assistant instructors so that we can break the class down into small groups, which frees me to walk around. A couple of other black belts worked with me, and I made sure they were communicating the right type of techniques.

The most valuable element in my Ju-Jutsu and Karate training was discipline, personal discipline. And the motivation that I have received was not necessarily to obtain a belt, but primarily to develop the skill. Whether a school gave out a belt or not, my motivation was to want to develop a high degree of skill.

Let me go back in history a little bit. After I became an instructor, I had the pleasure of working with Senseis that I still respect today, primarily for only one reason, because we all worked together. There was nobody trying to outdo the other. We were all trying to help each other. We had organized a system where at least once a month all the Senseis, in the Chicago area that I knew of, actually came into the shiais or tournaments we had. Sometimes there were interschool tournaments.

We had a board. In order to get on this board, we had these separate little events scheduled by a legitimate association. In other words you just couldn't come out of the clear blue sky and name yourself as head of an organization and say I'm so and so. We had organizations that accepted Kodokan Judo, USKA, and we had several Kung Fu organizations.

When I first came to the USKA, several clinics I went to were conducted by Robert A. Trias. These I thought were highly organized. (Editors note: Trias was the founder of the United States Karate Association and the Shorei Goju Karate system. He is widely acknowledged as the father of American Karate). I gained a great deal of knowledge and strength from going to them, because as a Sensei going to a strange place, I was often called upon to take over for a whole hour at some of these clinics. And these people were coming up for their black belt test. How would I run it? This caught me cold turkey and it really made me think and it helped me. And I realized that when he did this, his reason was to kind of test me, but also to teach me something. Then I met another Sensei I was quite impressed with. He was Sensei Yamashita. He used to teach out of Milwaukee and he came to many of our tournaments. Sensei Jimmie Jones [see Chapter XI] had some of his tournaments at McCormick Place and he also impressed me.

The Japan Karate Association (JKA) was in existence. [Editor's note: The JKA is the traditional Karate organization started by the founder of modern Japanese Karate, Gichin Funakoshi]. One of my good friends at that time was Sugiyama [Editor's note: Sugiyama was one of the first instructors to teach traditional Japanese Karate in the Midwest]. There weren't any Korean Instructors at that time. Sugiyama came to all of our meetings. It was left up to the instructors whether they wanted to come. Everyone was invited. During our monthly meeting, prior to any tournament, it was decided what each one of us would do: sit on a board, referee freestyle, decide on the type of trophies, and what the awards would be. Some people were responsible for having their students come and help the day before to tape fighting areas. So we were organized and one of the things that we clearly did when I had my tournament out at the Y was to have maximum participation from each of the legitimate Senseis who came to all the tournaments. We stressed that we'd all help each other. And I had Sensei Downs and myself, we had several tournaments up here in Evanston. For example, one time Sensei Jimmie Jones brought many of his co-workers from S&C Electric (at least 20 people) to turn over to me to teach because of the distance they would have to come to his dojo. These were the kinds of things that people worked together on. There was no jealousy. There were times when the other Senseis would welcome my students coming to visit them and my students would work with their classes, their instructors, then we might have about a half hour of freestyle competition at the end of the training session. Then that school would have refreshments and so forth. So we had a camaraderie within the martial arts community. I don't know whether it exists today, but we certainly had it then.

Some of my top students were William Matthews and Keith Taylor (Both men were members of international U.S. Karate teams). One other person who came to me from the Budo Kan Tang Soo Do [Way of the Chinese Hand] was Bill Downs. This was in the late 1970s. He was already a Shodan [first degree black belt] from Tang Soo Do and he wanted to come into the USKA. He wanted particularly to learn the Shorei [form of Okinawan Karate] system. Eventually we became friends and he wanted a partnership in our old school. Downs was a student of mine for a learning period, just to learn the Shorei system. He had prior accomplishments in his own right in martial arts.

One of the things that I feel I wanted all the years that I taught was to gain the respect of every student who came to me by my own doing, by the philosophy that I taught and by the way I taught it. And realizing that when a parent sent their child to me that they had the utmost respect that I would be teaching their child the right things. So I tried to impart the best knowledge of the martial arts that I could with respect, but I also demanded discipline of myself and, in particular, of the students in the school.

One of the main things I looked for was attendance. And one of the things I particularly looked for as a student began to come up in the rank was a sense of discipline and organization. For example, I could be in another room warming up and I used to teach my students that if I set the time for the class to start at 7:00 and I walk in the dojo at 7:15, that doesn't mean the students have to be laying on the floor, sitting around the wall waiting for me to walk in. Each person should start warming up. That person should know that they need to be doing something. So many times I've done this in school, I've actually tested the students and that includes the advanced students and I've actually waited to come into the class 15 minutes after the class started and found the students laying all over the floor, sitting around. I would explain to them that this is not martial arts. If the class starts at 7:00 and Sensei is talking, you need to know how to start your own class. And I stressed that whoever was the highest ranked person there could at least conduct the warm-up exercises in the class. So those are the kind of things that I would look for in a student. If a student was fighting and they were quick to anger, I knew that that student needed to be talked to because he needed to work on that. Because you're going to get some time when he might resort to anger and lose control and that's when other people get hurt.

To a person seeking martial arts training one of the things I would have them do is to meet one-on-one with the head instructor of that school to find out the history of that instructor, what that instructor intends to teach them and how the instructor intends to teach them. If during that one-on-one conversation, the would-be student began to feel that it's complex, that there are personal feelings and so forth, then maybe he should go somewhere else.

A lot of parents called me through the years, even since I've retired and I have always recommended to them that they try, if at all possible, try to stay away from contracts. Or, be very careful if they do get into a contract, because I've seen situations where a person signed a contract for their wife or something like that and the wife decides five months later she doesn't want it and so now here you are stuck with the contract. Also, if you go to a school and that person doesn't allow you to have at least one free class to see if you're going to like it, I think there's something wrong with the school. I think you need to go somewhere else.

During all the years that I've taught and practiced, one of the things I believe in as an instructor is in giving as much personal time to each student as is possible. It might be only once every two months, even though you may see them in class. Sometimes it's good to take that person in the office and ask him how does he think he's coming along. What does he think that he's gained or what could be helpful? Often times people help me by saying what they want.

I've found that in later years Sensei Downs and I went to our own report card. No. 1: we work with the students. We require them to be doing well, in their schoolwork, before they could come and participate in martial arts class. We kept our own personal report card and would give them an evaluation and this included attendance. We had critique sessions maybe once a week where we would talk with the students about the classes, maybe take about 10 or 15 minutes before and after the class to talk with them about how they thought they were progressing in class. And then we would do that on an individual basis. You find that some people come into class and they work very well with the group, but they are basically shy. So I think this is a very important thing for us as Senseis to work particularly hard with that individual. And when I used to find people like that I would have them come up beside me. I'd step aside and tell them in the next two or three minutes to take the class through some exercises while I

Louis Moseley (right), Bill Downs (left) and others Photo Courtesy of Louis Moseley

stand here working techniques. I was exposing them to leadership qualities without them realizing it. I think it's very important for a teacher to develop those who, hopefully, will remain with you to the end, so to speak, and will become good teachers. And I think part of our job is to give them the tools to work with by developing excellent skills and also the means to communicate this skill to others and that's through participation. So I believe in maximizing participation other than through the control of the Sensei.

I also have for years been a believer in working my students with their eyes closed, so they can feel themselves stumbling, faltering in their steps. Then I can tell them that their eyes are blind, closed, because they depend upon their eyes. But they really don't have the techniques deep seated in their minds, otherwise, their balance would be perfect. So many times, my students have told me this is one of the great things they like about practice. I make a student get up and the rest of us go along the wall and they get out there by themselves, I say `Now work your Kata.' Then I say, `Now do the same thing with your eyes closed.' Then I'll put an `X' mark on the floor and when the student comes back with his eyes closed, we'll see how close he came back to that line. So, these are little gimmicks, but they're things that I like. Those years I particularly enjoyed because I was surrounded by some fine people. And I hope it's that way today.

Sensei George Harris

Sensei George Harris was a member of America's first Olympic Judo team in 1964. Among many firsts, he was the first black international Judo competitor until the early 1970s. Harris is also world renowned as a Judo instructor, with over forty years experience.

Harris was born January 15, 1933 in Riddle, North Carolina. His first experience with the combative arts was at the age of 12 when he began boxing. He boxed until he was 19 years old. Harris entered the United States Air Force in 1952 as an air-medic. He became involved with the special services during the latter portion of that year. Harris began martial arts training in Judo at Travis Air Force base in California during this period.

Harris cross-trained in the martial arts, studying Karate, Aikido, Ju-jutsu, and Judo. For over 10 years Harris trained in Japan with some of the greatest Judo instructors of the day. He continues to train students and new teachers in traditional Judo. When he retires he will leave a legacy of having promoted Judo internationally in a regimented and disciplined fashion.

I began my martial arts training in California, at Travis Air Force Base In 1952. The Air Force sent me to school in Japan. I had to take Judo, Karate, Aikido, and Ju-jutsu. I did that for 10 years so I had quite a few instructors there: Kotani, Hosakowa, and Sensei Nakabayashi who helped me in my second national championship in the U.S. Quite a few other Senseis gave little tips here and there that helped. I went to Japan every year for 10 years for about three or four months each year.

The most valuable element that I have acquired from the martial arts thus far is discipline. To discipline myself. It became a way of life to me. Many times when I first started I thought about quitting because I was so big and to have little guys throw me around like that really upset me because I had been an amateur light heavy weight boxer. I could handle the little guys. It was the big guys that gave me problems. But in the Judo it was reversed.

The training that I received was different. In order for the Air Force to send me to Japan to take the Judo, I also had to take Karate , Aikido, and Taiho Ju-jutsu. So I had a real in-depth training of the martial arts and, as far as the Judo, I had the best. I had the world's greatest Senseis in Japan. And they got a big charge out of training me. I was the only black who came to Japan. I was obviously the biggest black they'd ever seen. And I took my beatings along with the ones that I gave out and kept coming back. My training was a lot different. And as far as the training that I give, I think Judo or any martial art instructor should train the total person. It shouldn't be how much money you can make off that person. It shouldn't be what kind of a champion that person can be, or can he make you look good. It should be what kind of a citizen that person is or can be. Is he the type who goes out and shows off in the school yard with other kids and shows them how good he is by bashing or pushing them around? Or is he the type of kid who will be very quiet and yet, if he sees a bully picking on someone else, he will go up and put his butt on the line?

I was on the 1964 Olympic team. That was the first Judo team to be in the Olympics. I tied for fourth. We had a light weight win a bronze. At that time American Judo was fifth in the world. Now, we're somewhere like twenty-something.

The road to the Olympics. Oh, God. They had not even said Judo would be in the Olympics when I started Judo. While I was training in Judo, they were talking about it, some of the Judo Senseis and administrators were trying to get Judo into the Olympics. And I kept thinking, wow, that would be great. I'd love to do that. I'd love to go there. I had heard of Jessie Owens. He was my idol, my hero, Jessie Owens, wow. So I finally got to meet him when I went to the Olympics in Tokyo. I said, 'You've been my hero all my young life. I've always wanted to meet you and I never thought I would be going to the Olympics and, of course,

George Harris at the 1964 Olympics Photo Courtesy of George Harris

here I am, meeting the great Jessie Owens.' He was an elderly man then, more or less. And he said, 'I'm just doing whatever anyone else would do.' I just had to get a picture taken with him. I see a lot of people that I idolize and I realize that if I've been to the Olympics, there are kids who'd do the same thing to me. So therefore, I should pattern my life so that a kid would like it and would understand it and I could be a role model for a kid.

The regimentation training for the Olympics involved a lot of sacrifice. I wasn't around to raise my kids, my three daughters, as much as I would like to have been, because I was traveling all over the world playing Judo. I didn't get the rank in the military like some of my friends, my co-workers, who were doing the same job that I was doing. I didn't get the retirement with the same rank that they did because I was running around the world playing Judo and they were there at their designated spot doing their job. So, that sacrifice cost me a lot of things. But I look at it today and say I gave that up because this is what I got for it. I got to be that champion. I got to go to the Olympics. I got all the accolades people put upon you as a champion. You're a hero. So I didn't make the retirement money that way. I make my money in doing clinics and just going to different tournaments.

When I was preparing, training for my first international competition it was at least five, six hours a day, five, six days a week. For local competition, I had a job. I was working. I did whatever I could when I could. Once I started, got a few wins under my belt, I knew which direction I wanted to go.

I was very impressed with the international competition and still am. I'm just sorry we didn't stay on the international ladder as we were at that time.

I was the only black competing internationally anywhere. Wherever I'd travel for a tournament, I was the hero before I even arrived, whether I competed or not, or lost or won. I finally met an African but he wasn't a player. He was a coach in 1964. I didn't see any international black players until about

When stationed in California during the early 1950's, a fellow Judo player and military man from the state of Texas extended an invitation for Sensei Harris to come down to Texas for a local competition. Upon arrival in Texas, Mr. Harris found that things were a lot different in the South. He was expected to adhere to the Jim Crow laws (written or unwritten). During his visit he experienced the humiliation of being refused service in a local restaurant, despite the fact that he raised his hand very vigorously. And then, to make the experience all the worst, while in transit back to the military base on a local bus line, Harris was forced to give up his front seat to a white woman, and sent to the rear of the bus. The experience left a very bitter taste with Harris. For years he refused the invitations of his fellow Judo players in Texas. When Harris finally did return in mid 1980s, he was greeted with this sign.

Photo Courtesy of George Harris.

1970s. There were a few national blacks in the black community, but they were not on the top national level.

In Judo I can speak really plainly. Judo I've watched evolve over the years. I think there was more throwing and clear, decisive, more classical Judo being played in the early years as opposed to now. Now Judo is played almost like a knockdown sport. Players don't necessarily go for the full throw. They just want to go and see if they can knock you down and to get a point because then they can win that way without committing themselves. They do not have finesse like those in the past. And it's gotten to the point where I think even the international community is beginning to try to change Judo because they're saying it looks almost like wrestling. And they've got enough wrestling going on. They want Judo to go back to the throwing.

It became very expensive to practice, too. Before, a Judo suit cost about six bucks for my size and all you needed was a high school mat, gym mat, or a tumbling mat. And every place wanted to try to do some Judo. And the military was very involved in Judo. So the military provided a lot of places and areas and got Judo going, even into the universities because a lot of the American G.I.s came back from overseas from Japan and Korea and places where they had trained. They brought Judo back and started clubs all over the country in their home towns. But it got so darn expensive. Now a Judo suit for myself can run anywhere from $200. It used to be $6 for me and about 2-3 dollars for a junior one. Now a junior has to pay $25 dollars for a suit.

The dedication is still there. I just think that the rules allowed the Judokas [Judo players] to not go after pure throws in Judo. In order to win in competition, you don't have to throw. You can knock the person down and win. So they would settle for knock down Judo. It was a rule change that caused it.

I ran schools in California, the Phillipines,

Massachusetts, New York, a couple in New York. I look for my students to have dedication. They also have to be self-motivated and they have to have that self-determination. It's difficult to motivate someone when you're telling them it's going to cost them $50 or $25 a month just to practice and then it's going to cost them so much for their uniform and so much for this or for that. They have to be self-motivated to want that.

I was even teaching before I went to the Olympics. I was constantly teaching. In Judo you can start teaching when you get to be a black belt. And so, I started in 1955 right after I became a black belt. I had to start helping the other beginners who were coming up.

Judo is a way of life to me and so it's not the competition that I think of as influencing, it's the competitor. I'm thinking of all the young minds I've influenced, all the young people that I've caused to change the direction of their lives. I could never count. I can't even mention. There's so many young kids I knew who've grown up to be young men. I've heard some of them since who are professionals, doctors, lawyers, that kind of thing. If I could influence anything, that's what I want to influence and that's what I've tried to influence. As far as the competitors, there have been some competitors that I've influenced, but that's not my focus. I'd rather teach young kids like I did tonight and try to get them to have a little self-confidence, get them to think of something else or someone else as a hero other than all the money makers. We don't make any money in Judo. But then Judo is a discipline like all the other martial arts. And if you can stand the discipline of the martial arts, then you can discipline yourself and that way you can avoid a lot of the pitfalls of life, smoking, drinking, drugs. All that is just strictly discipline. If you can discipline yourself those things don't become a part of you.

I've taught young kids who were wealthy. I've taught middle class kids and I've taught some poorer kids, ghetto kids. And I get just as big a charge out of teaching the ghetto kid. You take that anger and the energy that he has and you try to channel it into the martial arts. Try to channel it into discipline so that he can discipline himself, and he won't need the law. He won't need a prison to discipline. He won't need the police to discipline. He won't need a school teacher or an adult to discipline. He disciplines himself. That's the whole thing. That's life. We have the Great American Smokeout coming up . And it just amazes me that people can't stop smoking or can't stop drinking. There's nothing I cannot do if I want. All I have to do is put my mind to it because I've been trained to discipline myself. Judo has taught me to discipline myself. If everyone put that as a way of their life pattern, we wouldn't have all the things that are going on, prisons that are full of young black men, and young black men that are uneducated, and so forth and so on. And there wouldn't be every talented athlete who wants to be a money-making athlete, a football player or something. He'll be happy being a school teacher or teaching a team in a yard, in a playground or something where he can mold young men, where he can mold young minds.

I'd say after about 10 years in Judo, that's been my thrust, my responsibility. Once I learned what it means to be disciplined, to give way, to not let big objects or things or situations bowl me over or destroy my concentration or whatever, I went at whatever I wanted. I went after it with the zeal of a lion.

My thoughts are to watch a martial artist. He can be the greatest champion in the world. But if he doesn't give back to society, to the world, to the community, some of that information that he has learned or to try to help someone, then he hasn't learned anything. He didn't gain a thing. Now I've

UNITED STATES JUDO ASSOCIATION

CERTIFICATE OF
BLACK BELT JUDO RANK

Be it known that

GEORGE LEE HARRIS

has met all requirements established and set forth by the
United States Judo Association for promotion to the rank of

8TH DEGREE BLACK BELT

and is hereby certified at that rank by the USJA National Promotion Board
A high level of technical skill and knowledge of Judo have been demonstrated

As holder of this rank the individual is expected to continuously strive toward further
realization and ultimate achievement of the goals of Judo to promote the increased awareness
of Judo by others, and to exemplify the philosophy and discipline of Judo in all aspects of life

JULY 4, 1988

Date of Issue

CHAIRMAN OF THE BOARD

MEMBER OF THE BOARD

MEMBER OF THE BOARD

MEMBER OF THE BOARD

MEMBER OF THE BOARD

George Harris's eigth degree Judo black belt certificate.   Courtesy of George Harris.

watched some of the Karate champions. Chuck Norris, I see him getting involved with some of the young kids and trying to help. I hear him talking about what it's like to be a martial artist and what the responsibilities are that you take on when you become a champion or a martial artist. That's what I think a martial artist should be.

The advice I give to a person seeking martial arts training is to make sure that you pick the martial art for the right reason. If you're picking it so that you can go out and be the toughest guy in the world or you're picking it so that you won't have to worry about somebody picking on you or bugging you or attacking you—those are all the wrong reasons. If you're picking it for the discipline, to better yourself, to see if you can be the best that you can be—all those things, yeah, okay. Now, when you are the best that you can be, the things that I was just mentioning will come along. You won't have to worry about the person picking on you. Many times I've had people who have tried to pick on me and I've walked away from them because I didn't need to prove anything. And that's what I said to them. I don't have to prove anything to you. All I can tell you is don't touch me. Now, if you touch me, you're going to put yourself in jeopardy. I'm going to defend myself but only if you touch me. Words won't bother me at all. Call me all the names you want. So that's the way I've run my life. I've been called names. I came up in the fifties when they called me all kinds of outrageous names. But that didn't bother me. I knew who I was and I knew what I could do.

People see all this stuff in the movies and they think that they can do that. They never think that a lot of that stuff is trick photography. It's all make-believe. The movies are nothing but make-believe. There are many reasons that people take the martial arts, some are not good reasons. And nothing will come of it. They're looking to become super-heroes or supermen in 10 easy lessons. I've seen where these different schools have taken a six-year-old and made him a black belt. That's being a little farfetched. Sure, you're making money off that. But

George Harris with practice partner. Photo Courtesy of George Harris.

I think that's not really letting the kid develop. You've tried to develop his skill but you haven't developed his mind, haven't told him what he has to do, what responsibilities go along with it.

If you are an instructor and your kids' rank goes yellow, purple, green, brown, black and then your adults' ranks go the same way. Okay. But you've got to let the kid know that his black belt is not equivalent to the adult black belt. His is a kid's black belt. But see, that causes confusion in the young mind. They don't understand that. Why isn't my black belt the same as his black belt? And their parents are really illiterate about it. They understand their kid is 8 years old and he's a black belt. Well, lah dee da. Great. Does that mean maybe he's top in the 8-year-olds in that school, in that system? Or does it mean that he's as tough or as knowledgeable as an adult black belt? No way. He doesn't have the speed. He doesn't have the strength, the agility. He doesn't have all those things that an adult would have.

I was talking to a kid tonight in the Judo class. He wanted to know why he couldn't be a black belt. And I said, You have 12 degrees in your junior rank. You can go all the way to 12 degrees, which is purple. And then from there, if you're old enough as a purple belt, at sixteen, you can become a brown belt. At seventeen, you can become a black belt. But you're an adult black belt. You're going to fight as an adult. You'll fight an adult black belt. You're not going to wear an adult black belt and fight a junior. That's not the way the game goes.

We keep the rank so that you don't confuse the young mind. That's the bad thing I find out about all the different martial arts, Judo included. They don't educate the young mind, train the young mind in the martial arts and all of the things about it as they go along. They are so busy in trying to train them in different moves, how to move this way, how to do this, how to strike that, how to throw here. They don't really get their minds, tell them, you're still a junior.

George Harris with Judo professor. Photo Courtesy of George Harris.

It wasn't always that way. It got that way when different martial artists started to bastardize their sport, to sell it for money. They were trying to make money. Every time the kid got promoted the parents paid another $25, $35, $50. And all of a sudden, this kid, he's had eight, nine promotions and he's now a black belt. That parent has paid for that. And some schools advertise that. We can make you a black belt in six months. That's impossible because each individual is different. And if you don't have it, if you're a klutz, you're a klutz. It takes a lot of years, a lot of training, a lot of practice, a lot of sacrifice. I can't even tell you of the sacrifice that it takes. It takes an enormous amount of sacrifice. And most people are not willing to do that. They want instant gratification. Right now. Even if they have to buy it.

I think we should all try to physically and mentally prepare ourselves for life. A lot of people either do one or the other, and some do neither. They don't prepare themselves for life. They think that the world owes them a living. The world doesn't owe you crap. Anything you want, you are going to have to go out and get it. And the way you're going to get it, is not with a gun, but you're going to have to earn it because you want whatever you get to be respected and you want others to respect you. No one's going to respect you with a gun except the person you rob. You can't rob the whole world. I see these kids writing graffiti (their name and so forth) all over walls. Why are they doing that? I asked my own kids once, why would any kid, climb up on the side of a 747 just to write his initials? And my kid looked at me and said, 'Oh, Dad, he'd be famous.' People are going to remember it. And I said, 'You know what, people are going to remember me. And I never wrote my name on anything that didn't belong to me. I've never defaced anyone else's property. Don't you think people are going to remember me? Because I did something worthwhile. You do something good, it doesn't have to be something outstanding or great.' Do something good for another human being. You'll be remembered. That's my philosophy.

I'm still constantly giving back to the martial arts as I'm constantly learning. Every day I learn something new about my sport, my particular martial art. And every day, I try to give back something, whether it's in martial arts or in my every day life using my martial arts training, my Judo philosophy to give way, to redirect your energy. That's just the way I am.

I haven't always been this way. I tell people, when you're a competitor, you're selfish, you don't give anything. All you want to do is take, to receive, to get. It's after you finish your competitive career that if you've learned anything from your sport, that's when you find out you're trying to give back.

Strong competitors like Preston Baker (middle) were taught by Black Pioneers (Chuck Norris on left) Photo Courtesy of Louis Moseley

Professor Ronald Duncan

Professor Ronald Duncan is widely recognized as the "Father of American Ninjutsu." His 50 plus years of martial arts experience has canvassed a great number of combative art forms both occidental and oriental. For almost 40 years he has imparted his knowledge to thousands of students and influenced many of the prominent martial artists of today.

Duncan was born in the Republic of Panama in 1937. He began his martial arts training in boxing at age 6 in Panama City. Duncan's formal training in martial arts began in 1948, in Ju-jutsu, under the instruction of the legendary Charlie Neal. He has also trained under other prominent martial artists such as Earnie Cates, Tatsuo Uzaki and the late Donn Draeger.

As an ambassador of the martial arts Duncan has been featured numerous times in martial arts magazines (Black Belt, Official Karate, Warriors, World Professional Karate, and others). He has also appeared on various national television programs such as "Thrillseekers," "Interface," and ABC's "Wide World of Sports."

Duncan continues to actively teach and promote the martial arts internationally. His emphasis remains combat realism.

I started off in the martial arts training, if you want to consider boxing a martial art, at 6 years old. My first instructor was a boxing instructor, Earnest Reed. He was a professional fighter. He was from the same hometown as Roberto Duran.

In 1948, I began studying Chi Chitsu, the art of nerve pinching.

My first Ju-jutsu instructor was Charles Neal. Neal was a pioneer martial artist in the United States, a black instructor, in Portsmouth, Virginia. He founded one of the first martial arts schools in the United States around 1948. It was called the Portsmouth Authentic Judo Club.

There were other significant instructors. The legendary Major Donn Draeger. He wrote many books. He's the foremost historian of modern day martial arts. He was a major in the Marine Corps and he did a lot to establish the martial arts in the Tidewater area in Portsmouth, Virginia and I consider him one of my mentors, also. He's now deceased.

I was not only satisfied with my training, but I considered it a privilege that I was allowed to train in the martial arts. Because back in those days there weren't many doors open to black instructors, black practitioners, black students. So I was privileged to be given the opportunity to pursue a life-long dream.

The doors began to open for black practitioners at the end of the second World War, when General McArthur occupied Japan. Black servicemen were stationed over there after the war. Some got involved in those art forms which were allowed to flourish. When Japan capitulated, most of the martial arts institutions were shut down in Japan. So around 1948, 1949 black servicemen began with Judo, just Judo. Many of these black servicemen studying Judo were Airforce individuals. And the Strategic Air Command was just beginning to be founded and as part of their curriculum, they were required to study martial arts. I don't know the exact number of blacks who studied formally. But I've met some.

The most valuable element that I've obtained was the ability to focus. It allowed me a springboard for excellence in my life, in my career. Ever since that time, I have gained a lot through understanding myself and gaining a degree of self-control. I can control my own soul, my destiny, through the discipline that I gained through the martial arts. I can deal with the day-to-day instances of life, through my pain, and win. Not only physically, but spiritually, intellectually, and psychologically.

I first began teaching martial arts in October of 1957 at the Portsmouth Virginia Naval Station. I

Professor Ronald Duncan. Photo Courtesy of Ronald Duncan.

was a marine but I was asked by my commanding officer to teach the seagoing marines. The seagoing marines were a contingent of maybe 100 men who were serving aboard Navy ships as military policemen.

I opened my first school in 1959: St. John's Recreation Center, Brooklyn, New York. It wasn't really my school, but the center allowed us to train. Many of the black pioneer instructors were there, people such as Elliot Farrell. My first dojo that I opened under my own auspices in 1964 was called the Bushido School of Self-Defense in Brooklyn, New York. Then I relocated to this building that houses Queens Village Pistol and Rifle Range in 1980 and I've been here ever since. But I have affiliated schools around the world.

What I look for in my martial arts students is character, first of all. I run all my schools that way. I screen every student that comes in to me. I put them to test before I accept them in any of my schools.

I don't run a commercial school because I don't make a living from the martial arts. I've been teaching martial arts in New York since 1959 and the martial arts will always be an avocation, whereas I taught martial arts in the evenings and on weekends. But I do have a profession. I'm a highly trained, confidential, specialized investigator, which I still am today.

I've influenced people such as George Coefield, Thomas LaPuppet, and Mfundishi Maasi, Moses Powell, you name it, Fred Hamilton, Cleofus Jacobs, Ron Van Clief. And James Noreiga from Ninja Magazine, and Bill Vasquez, who is also well known in the Ninja art form, Rich Whittington, people who have become acclaimed. People across the country and other countries. Those are the names that come to mind. These are people that I've influenced and these people can attest to that, in one form or another. I'm not claiming any ownership on all these people, but guys like Ed Quentin Garden, some of the people that I trained privately, but not the public at large.

When we speak of yesterday, we've got to look in terms of the martial artists who were studying in the 1950s and 1960s. Now we are in the 1990s. When we speak of yesterday I like to go back, say, to round 1956. Which gives us all of four decades. The difference between the martial artists today and the martial artists then is that we had a narrower path to follow. Things were more traditional. Things were more geared toward the cultural aspect of whatever art form we embraced, Chinese, Japanese, Korean, Hindu, whatever the case might be. There was a higher level of regimentation. It was an either/or, whether you do it or not. The difference then was that we trained harder. There wasn't that much information disseminated. There were a lot of restrictions. There was a lot of secrecy. There was a lot of mystique that surrounded these art forms and as the years progressed, martial arts became more and more eclectic. People began to study by being in the military, learning from instructors under all kinds of conditions. The martial artists today are a lot more superior than the martial artists of yesterday, despite the fact that there's not the same level of regimentation.

Even on the intellectual level. It's because there's been more information disseminated over the years. There's more of a cross culture, intermingling of styles. As a result, even in the Orient, China, Japan, wherever, the same occurred. The difference then was that with the restrictive regimentation, the practitioners were focused and they were effective and they had greater respect. A large mass of the population was exposed to the martial arts. If a guy was studying a martial arts form and he had a black belt, he was looked upon as some sort of mysterious figure. A lot of respect went along with it. But as the years progressed, that mystique, that veil sort of evaporated, so more people had access to the art form. More people could read about it. Practitioners today are geared more toward a sporting aspect of the martial arts form as opposed to those of yesteryear. When I say sporting aspect, they're more tournament oriented. And

I think that egos today are slightly more inflated that the egos of yesterday.

Back in the early days we were very physical martial artists. In every generation you're going to find those individuals who are either spiritually inclined, those who are intellectually inclined, those who are physically inclined, or those who would prefer to be martial arts buffs. Then you'll have those individuals who are a combination of two or three. It's rare to find an individual who's a combination of all. It's a self-effacing, self-sacrificial mode of existence.

I'm not guided through media creation, or what is fed or disseminated to the public at large. I don't think there are any great martial artists that ever existed for the simple reason that martial arts is a very individual, personalized experience. The greatest martial artist is that individual who has gained total control over his existence, over himself. I don't think there's a single human being in this society today who can claim to have gained total control over self because of the pull, to and fro, back and forth by the various aspects that we are bombarded with in day-to-day living. I don't think the greatest martial artist has been found yet. Just like the greatest boxer or athlete hasn't been found yet. Some individuals excel at a certain time and in certain areas so they garner the public's attention. So the public and media create this greatness of people. There's no man under the sun, nor ever there has been a man under the sun, that you can call the greatest anything.

I look at life realistically. By looking at life realistically I don't create delusions about what a martial artist is to expect. I try not to teach people what they think they need to know, but what I know from my experiences of dealing with situations I teach them what they need to know and what they need to learn. And from that point on they develop individually. I allow my students to take the seeds that I implant into them to develop and grow, just like leaves and the branch of a tree. That's how come I've helped to create some great martial

Ron Duncan states that he has influenced many people, such as Mfundishi Maasi.

Photo Courtesy of Mfundishi Maasi.

artists. Because I don't try to control their actions.

The advice that I would give anybody seeking martial arts training today is to be sure in his or her life that martial arts is going to be an area of exploration that they will want to devote time and energy and, of course, money to. And I tell this to people coming into my school. If you're not ready, I don't want your money. Just leave. Go someplace else. I tell them before they look for martial arts schools to know what they want to study. No. 1, and why they want to study martial arts, No. 2. What do they plan to derive and gain from the sacrifice? And what do they intend to do with it to benefit themselves, their families, society, and mankind at large? Let's face it. When we speak in terms of martial arts on the physical level, the physical level of combat is what we call the animalistic type. That's the lowest level of combat, isn't it? But what's being waged on society today is a psychological attack of the minds of the people. So how do you deal effectively with a psychological attack with people who try to control you economically, to instill fear, off-balance you because of economics? People have to look to gain from the martial arts the furthest levels from which they can exist peacefully and respectfully and to gain a level of control of themselves, their families, their destinies to live peacefully and happily.

My philosophy of life is that nothing happens without a reason, that no man on this planet, no matter what his endeavor happens to be, is greater than the greater God. And my philosophy is that anything that we do is a gift to us from the supreme creator. And life is a series of strategies, offenses, defenses in man's quest for survival. And since survival is a key word today in this world at large, my philosophy is to be strong, to maintain yourself, a sense of integrity, under whatever set of circumstances. I believe we should not only project, but live a life of honesty, respect, dignity, and love for our fellow man. I'd like to think that once these principles are incorporated into people's day-to-day living, I think we'll have a better society by and large, and eliminate greed, hatred, prejudice, bigotry, all this violence. I think we'll eliminate this dissecting of community by creating elements within the community, especially the black community, to create a decadent type of existence, repressive existence. As black people, we have to learn to recognize these things, to realize trends that have been set for us to follow are merely traps, which regress our roles and our potentials into the centuries that are coming.

I've gotten out of the martial arts exactly the things that I'm telling you. I live it. I live those things. I've given a lot back to the martial arts community because I've given back a lot to a lot of people that I have trained. I've been able to see them disseminate information. I've given a lot of my time to the martial arts. I have shared my knowledge, my wisdom, my gifts, to many in the martial arts community. I actually am not retired. Just the idea to share, and the idea of sharing is to see, to benefit my fellow man. I'm still giving back to the martial arts.

We've got to get back to the principles. An individual can study under the most prolific martial artists in existence and gain knowledge and wisdom and still, there has to be that inner voice, that inner self, what we call that natural, original face that nobody will see, that dictates what we do and what we do not do. A lot of individuals in the martial arts are magnificent specimens, great fighters, great tacticians, but that something is lacking, that spirituality is lacking, that spirituality which guides us all. That's why they're falling left, right, and center. Far too many martial artists believe that hype about themselves.

I would like to see the martial arts disseminated in a way that can be not only beneficial to the public at large, but without offending their intellect, their sensitivities, and their common sense. I would like to see the martial arts not only as this physical thing, but the thing that's going to improve the character and the intellect of the people at large so that we can evolve, because we have a long way to go as people. We're still in the evolutionary stage and I feel that martial arts is one of the ways in which a person with that basic concept can achieve and succeed. They can become a great physician, a great lawyer, a great teacher, a great janitor, a great tailor, whatever it is they set out to do. It will give them the springboard, the focus, to allow them to excel.

When we speak in terms of pioneers, you have to think in terms of Staff Sergeant George Harris, who's still alive and lives up in Westchester County. He represented the United States in Judo. Sergeant Lyndon Williams and Sergeant Sam Boone, are still around. When we speak in terms of the pioneers we had Elliot Farrell, a black man, a Ju-jutsu guy, a Judo guy. Elliot was teaching martial arts before I was. Elliot was teaching martial arts when he first got out of the Marine Corps in the Second World War. The Marine Corps began to recruit black men in 1943. And Sergeant Jones, we called him Judo Jones, Sergeant Gaslow, and Sergeant Martinez. These men were trained with white Marines, down at camp Lajeunne in North Carolina to go fight the Japanese. This was in 1943, 1944, and 1945. Now that in itself was an accomplishment and an achievement because the Marines didn't go through boot camp together. We went through what's called Mudford Point Marines. The Marine Corps was segregated, until President Truman drew up those barracks. Then we had Charles Neal, my Sensei in Ju-jutsu. He went through the ranks of police lieutenant in Portsmouth, Virginia and became very prominent. Sensei Charlie Neal also began to teach Marines when he went in at the end of the Second War and during the Korean War. When the Korean War broke out, Sensei Neal was aboard ship, training the troops going back and forth to Korea in hand-to-hand combat, what you call combative methods.

And then we had Charles Elmore. He's still around. He's alive, in his 70s now. And was self-taught and teaching Ju-jutsu before anyone would touch him to teach him. He was teaching Ju-jutsu in 1953, 1954, 1955, 1956. And then the rest of the folks around began to teach like in 1960 and so forth.

When we speak in terms of who the pioneers are nobody wants to mention these pioneers. I feel obligated to mention these men. Without them teaching in these little obscure places like YMCAs and little gyms and down in the basements and shoestores in back, there wouldn't be any black martial arts in this country today. They influenced a lot of people out here in the United States and places like Trinidad, Jamaica, Panama and Nicaragua, where black men involved in teaching military troops in the Second War in those areas, learned at that time in those YMCAs too.

When we're speaking in terms of black existence in martial arts we have to look at the art form of Bombay, originally a Nigerian art form, which opened thousands of combative systems that are actually African. The ingredients of Capoeira are an art form that came out of Africa. I know that because I have students in Africa, I have affiliations in Africa, which document the facts about the martial arts. Capoeira is a Portuguese word out of Brazil.

When you speak in terms of the black-skinned man creating a martial art, you will find dark-skinned, black Indians teaching martial arts over in one of the places called Kinowa in India, which has been in existence for thousands of years.

Bruce Lee and all these people, they are created by the media. The media- created people are not going to save you in a dark alley if you have to fight for your life. I know what I'm talking about because I walk that fine line every day as an investigator on the street in the toughest neighborhoods. Nobody cares who you are out on the street. You could be a 20th degree Black Belt. They don't care. They'll take you on if you're not ready. That's how I look at martial arts. You've got to be there. You've got to witness an experience. I bring a lot of my experiences into the dojo to teach my students. A lot of those guys are military and law enforcement guys. I'm now a certified law enforcement instructor. I'm also a certified firearms instructor.

I'm a master shooter: pistols, rifles, and shotguns. I'm one of the only certified knife throwers left in this country. And in addition to all I'm doing, I'm now teaching my students counterintelligence methods, electronic surveillance.

I'm telling you like it is. I don't pretend. I can back it up. That's my philosophy. You've got to walk to walk, and talk to talk. If somebody doesn't believe it can be done, then I say let's do it and I'll show you. If you can match it, match it. If you can't then let me do it. That's how I've stood for all these years in martial arts training. I don't believe in hype. I'm never satisfied. Never, ever satisfied. At age 56 I'm still training whenever I can.

Sensei James Cheatham

As told by his senior student Mfundishi Maasi

Sensei James Cheatham was born in New Jersey in 1934. He was the son of a famous Reverend, a one-time boxer out of New Jersey who had over 100 professional fights. Cheatham, a man well ahead of his time, was one of the first black martial arts instructors to attempt to galvanize the black martial arts community along the Eastern seaboard. He influenced the martial arts community for more than a decade.

Cheatham was in the forefront in addressing the political issues of the late 1950s and early 1960s that pertained to blacks. Politically, James Cheatham followed the teachings of the Nation of Islam. James Cheatham leaves the legacy of an innovator. Within the realm of the martial arts, he incorporated many techniques and theories from martial arts systems other than Karate. Cheatham died in a plane accident while flying solo as a novice pilot in June 1966.

James Cheatham began his martial arts training in about 1954 or 1955 in the art of Shito Ryu Karate under Wallace Reumann. He was a truck driver. He made light deliveries. Cheatham had some Judo training prior to Karate .

I think with Chea Chea, that's what most people called him, gaining the art, learning the art, coming in contact with the art, I think it pressed a button somewhere. As far as history, there have been no martial artists who required such a minimum of formalized teaching. And once that center was open he just seemed to draw from all sources. He was that kind of person. He was an innovator. Last year I found out that his father was a professional boxer. Reverend Cheatham had over 100 some fights and it really was evident in Chea Chea's style of fighting because when we used to go to tournaments in the 1960s they'd say to us, `You all are not really Karate men. You're more like boxers and fighters, street fighters.' And now that's what everybody wants to be. Before it was a curse. Now it's a blessing. When I became familiar with Bruce Lee, and I respect him highly, but everything that he said, I heard Chea Chea say it years ago. For me, the father of full contact fighting in America was James Cheatham because when we went to tournaments and we fought our particular style, they told us that we were coming in too hard, had to tone it down. We weren't making malicious contact. It was just in the dojo we trained to make contact and if you didn't block, you were hit. It was as simple as that. If you couldn't handle that, you didn't go on the floor, that's all.

He used to go to tournaments in New York City. We ran into some good fighters over there, but I must say, they were never happy to have to fight us because we came with a rough-and-ready brand of fighting and we were disqualified most of the time. The tournament referees and officials would tell us we weren't using what they considered Karate techniques. They wanted us to lock and hold. No, we don't do that. We're not using their standard of focus. We're going to snap through. We just did what we were trained to do. They wouldn't recognize the points and we would score in the way we were trained to do and they'd say, `You're disqualified.' And we'd say, `We won anyway and see you next time.'

There was a sign facing you as you came through the door and many people comment about this statement, that it was bravado. But it wasn't really that. Chea Chea welcomed anyone to come to the school. You'd come and observe. He wasn't the kind of person who had secret techniques that he had to hide from you. But if you made comments about your level of skill or the lack of skill that you saw, or fooled yourself into believing that's what you saw, then the sign said, 'If you feel that your techniques are strong enough, if you've got what it takes, feel free to indulge in Randori (free fighting).' Sometimes he used the Judo term for a Karate term and it really meant Kumite (Sparring). So that was the type of school we had, free, open, no secrets, no discrimination. Anyone could come and fight and spar as long as they really brought their guts and not just their mouth and attitude. It was really the hallmark of the school.

Sensei James Cheatham. Photo Courtesy of Mfundishi Maasi.

He exuded self-confidence, in spite of the fact that he had a slight stammer. It's ironic that he had a stammer, because he was anything other that an uptight, stammering, stuttering person. He seemed to have a high level of energy and it would sometimes try to come out, everything at the same time. He had a high level of confidence and he advocated martial arts training, at that time Karate training. As he would say, be real and know who you are. To be real, bottom line, was what you were, find out what that was and then be it and not compromise yourself. That was his principle. So I would have to say, I don't know how much of that he brought to the art, but I noticed that as being his dominant characteristic, the thing he pushed most vigorously.

He had one school in two locations. The first school was at 830 Broad Street. He closed it down and moved further down Broad Street in Newark, New Jersey. The second school was at 913 Broad Street, just down the street, the opposite side. We got to the place around 1964, 1965.

We fought hard. We may not have appeared as flashy, but we fought harder and our techniques were authentic because Chea Chea was a stickler for that. He would often say, never push. Where you can push, you can always punch. That was his concept. Even if you get inside and you're jockeying for position with little room, he wanted you to punch him away from you, not push him away. So that was really his thing, to be authentic. In his estimation a black belt should be able to defend himself or herself against someone wielding a stick, a razor, a knife, or a gun, if it was close enough. His concept was to be able to defend empty hand against empty hand or against weapon hand.

Just about anyone could join us and he would give them a chance. Then if you didn't have the warrior spirit, he would work with you, but he wouldn't be as focused. He had his pets, those who he knew had what he was looking for. And then you caught hell because you had to be exactly what he wanted you to be. A kick had to be just where it was supposed to be and if it failed to be there, then that was a cardinal sin, because he relied upon you to teach the lower belts. Once he placed the confidence in you to guide and shape the class, then you didn't shave it off, didn't cut it short.

When you talk to martial artists, you can get into the ego thing. I would say he influenced, in a spiritual way, in a brotherly way, African-American martial artists in the New York-New Jersey area in the way that he influenced Talo-naa and his group in Chicago. Even the non-black martial artists gained from him but would never admit it. He was very sharp. He carried himself with a dignity and authority, but he wasn't heavy handed with it. He stayed within his own space.

He was very political about power for black people. Very much so. In fact all of his black top guns, the black black belts were affiliated with the Nation of Islam. I was the first brother to train the Nation of Islam mosque, 25 North New Jersey. He didn't require it. But he influenced me to become a Muslim, to have knowledge of self. Part of being yourself was to have a historical knowledge of yourself. Now they would say the ethnic knowledge of yourself.

Some of his student's were: Prentiss Newton, who's now maybe chief of detectives with the Essex County prosecutor's office. I know he's due for a promotion. But he's been a detective for some time. Kareem Allah came through the K system. Larry Hazard is the boxing commissioner for the state of New Jersey. In fact, I directly trained Larry during the Saturday class. Chea Chea never taught on Saturdays. I taught on Saturdays, but naturally, he was Larry's teacher. The energy in the school was Chea Chea's and he influenced Larry. A brother, Ibretheem Shariff, has been rewarded many times by various citizen groups in Essex County, New Jersey, for his work with children and community work, things of that nature.

Chea Chea was not a big man. He was 5'9", 5'10" at max, 145, maybe 150 pounds when he was at his heaviest. But the way he was constructed (he wasn't massive, he was very wiry), his hands and arms were large and his legs and feet were large. So he could easily gain momentum in a snap. He could gain momentum to tear through.

Also he had a type of courage that was amazing. I have a picture of him putting his fingers through three cement slabs, three concrete cinders. Back then no one ever worked with fingers. Through his association with Allen Lee, who was his good friend and partner, he began to investigate the use of fingers. I remember the day he did it. I saw him setting up in the back room. He didn't invite anybody to watch. But we black belts had access to him. He just snapped right through with no hesitation. No hesitation, no fear, no bravado. Just boom and he swept up the pieces and that was the end of it. He was about showing it. He used to have a little saying that Shodan [first degree black belt] meant "to show." If you're a Shodan, show it. At that point there was no more talk, you're a Shodan. His Shodans showed it. His thing was his green belts could beat black belts. His brown belts could beat higher level black belts. And his black belts 'had it that way,' to use the vernacular of the youngsters nowadays. And at that time and because of his intensity and because we weren't trapped in that classical thing, we actually 'had it that way.'

His basic philosophy of life was to always check yourself out. To know where you're coming from and to be yourself. Those were the two things he pushed all the time. He would often say, `That, kid, that was kind of sloppy. You need to dig yourself. You need to check yourself out.' No long, drawn out technical dissertation. He was very informal.

My promotion to black belt, we knew it was in the air for some time. I walked into the dojo one evening and he was standing with his back to me, near the case where he kept the belts and uniforms (the gis). As I walked in he turned around and threw the black belt at me, boom. He said, 'Put it on.' I remember saying, 'I don't know if I'm ready for this.' He said, 'I didn't ask you. I told you to put it on.' Now that was the promotion right there. I walked out on the floor with it and that was it. So he was very informal. But he would test you over and over and over for months ahead of time. The process would already be done by the time the promotion took place. Very informal. We utilized a bow, but we didn't use Japanese terminology.

The things he discussed then,his application of technique, I'm seeing now. I remember one day he swept Kareem Allah out of the air. Kareem was a great leaper, good with the side kick. Chea Chea swept a crescent kick back. Just slapped it in mid-air with his foot. And jumped. I looked. The timing was impeccable. It was the timing. No forethought, no, 'I'm going to set him up and I've got him.' That was just the way that he moved. I feel he was a natural because he didn't waste much time. I think he made black belt in nine months. He was authentic because Chea Chea was well known for being a strong fighter and not arrogant, but just very confident. And he demanded that of everyone, If you were one of his guns, green belt, brown belt, or black, you had to be able to hold your own. It didn't mean that you didn't lose. It meant that you did everything that you had to do to win but if your opponent was better, then that was it. But if he saw you slacking off or hanging back, he let you know. He'd take you back to the dojo and he'd just spar with you, show you where your mistakes were.

When he was snatched away from us he was in the midst of several business deals. He was getting a pilot's license to fly back and forth to the Caribbean for some things he was working on. He was involved with Grand Master Allan Lee importing uniforms that were made in China, things of that nature. So he was in the midst of several deals, including a jewelry business. He was partners in a transmission shop. So he was pretty spread out. Prentiss and I, we taught most of the time the last month or two before he died.

I think Chea Chea got confidence and self knowledge out of the martial arts. It's like a cliche...the self knowledge and the opportunity to influence people's lives. I really, really saw that in him, that he had an interest in people beyond their martial skills. It was always about bettering your circumstances, upgrading yourself, always about that.

He gave to the martial arts community for those who remember back that far and will admit it, a commitment to excellence in practice and execution and the way that he presented himself. He was meticulous about certain things like the way that you rolled your gi and the way you carried it. You don't ball it up, wrap your belt. For him it was an honor to be a martial artist, or Karate man, as we called it. And he carried himself that way. And just through that silent energy, he inspired all his students in a way that suggested strength and dignity combined. And yet he had a funny side, he had a clown side. But you didn't see that too often. In terms of the art, no, you didn't see that. But if you went to a picnic or barbecue or something like that, then he would joke, then he was `Yeah, The Cheach.' If you didn't know him you couldn't associate him with the stern taskmaster. But you could hang out with him on Sunday and when you came to the advanced class on Tuesday, don't look for that. When you walk through, he'd say, `On the floor, you're late.'

He's still a legend in the Newark area. There are people who claim they trained under him. I just listen to them. You hear them talking. So he's recognized among old-timers and the youngsters who are hooked into someone who trained back then. No, he hasn't been forgotten.

I remember, we observed him in a match one evening. Julius Dudley, an Army lieutenant who trained in Korea for a while, came into the school one evening. He wanted to work out. He was from the old Tang Soo Do school, black piping around the gi, and the thick belt, it looked blue or sort of black and kicks that shot straight up in the air. At that time he was a typical Korean fighter, no hands, but his kicks were like, boom, wow. He was a bit

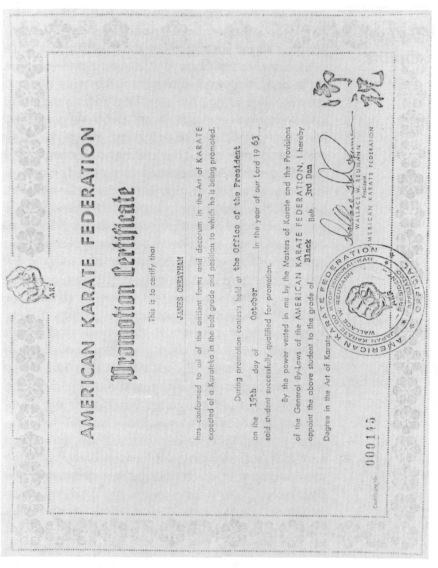

James Cheatham's third degree black belt certificate Courtesy of Mfundishi Maasi

cocky. He was a young man. He asked Chea Chea, `You want to spar?' and Chea Chea said, `Alright.' They sparred and Dudley was coming in with BANG and Chea Chea just sidestepped. As I look back, and I understand about his father's influence having some effect, the shuffling and the slipping and sweeping the platform leg and things like that, just saying, no, 'You're not going to kick me that easily with that stiff kick. You have to loosen up a bit.' And that's what he told him after the match. He said, `Good kicks, but just too stiff. I saw them coming, like a steel rod, you have to bend a little more.' He told him about the bamboo thing and how you bend and flow. But there was no anger and no defensiveness when he said, `Okay, I'll spar.' And there was no anger or hostility or maliciousness when he went on the floor with him. He had just real good technique. His philosophy, in sparring, was you bow in, score the first point, establish the speed. Then you dominate and just stay on the person. You just control the floor. If you don't want him to kick, you don't let him kick. Then you would converse, you'd spar back and forth.

I saw him angry once. We were in New York City in Manhattan. We were sitting in a restaurant and there was a problem with some folks in there. When the officers came in, they came straight to us. It was Chea Chea, Prentiss, and another brother. His attitude was like, `Look, I don't even want to hear it. You go catch some crooks. Don't bother me.' And it was hard. It was cold. It was direct. And they left him alone. He was pretty soft-spoken. But he had a way of communicating.

We were in Canada at a tournament and prior to the finals each Sensei had to recite his pedigree. Chea Chea, he had a bit of a stammer, he stood up, `M-my name's James Cheatham and I come from n-north New Jersey and you'll know my rank by the way m-my m-men fight here tonight.' The crowd was stunned. He was a little hyperactive sometimes, but he always got his point across. And those were our marching orders . We would distinguish him by the way we fight. Because he always gave his all, everything. You never got the impression that it was about trying to impress anybody. It was always about working with this person or that person. He gave it all to you. He never hid anything. He never said there's some secret things I can't show you, there's a Kata I might show you 10 years from now. He would say, 'Look, this is it, go to work. But don't slouch.'

Robert Brown (left, back row) with Bob McNutt (right, back row) with students. Courtesy of Robert Brown.

Sensei Robert Brown

Sensei Robert Brown owned and operated one of the first black commercial martial arts schools in the Chicagoland area. He maintained a reputation as a serious Karate instructor offering a holistic approach to those who trained under him.

Brown, a retired police officer, was born in Chicago, Illinois in 1933. After his military service Brown began studying Judo in 1959. He sustained a shoulder separation, which ended his Judo aspirations. In 1960 Brown started to study Karate under Chicago's famous John (Count Dante) Keehan. Brown is a staunch believer in strong basics and the constant creation of psychological challenges for those who train in the martial arts. Brown's training philosophy is that "Nothing is impossible, if you are willing to pay the price."

I started my study of martial arts in 1959. Originally, I started in Judo. My first instructor was a gentlemen by the name of Mas Tamura. He was a sixth degree black belt Judo man and he ran the old Ju-jutsu Institute on Van Buren Street in Chicago. And after that, I studied Aikido with Commander Kramer. He was only in Chicago for a short time. Right after that I began my study of Karate and my first instructor was John Keehan, later to become Count Dante. I studied with John, up until around 1964 and I was a member of the United States Karate Association, and I received my Shodan [first degree black belt] from him.

My training was pretty thorough and it was kind of rough. John was a perfectionist. John was a person who believed you had to be physically perfect and in martial arts you had to know the martial arts. It started with the very basics and continued on through. You progressed as far as your abilities took you.

The most important thing was personal drive. You learn to never quit, to never give up, never taste defeat, just keep going. We learned that any man could succeed if he was willing to pay the price and that was one of the things that carried over into my life. That was one of the things I tried to impart to my students.

I look back over the guys that came along, Tolo-Naa, Jimmie Jones. There was Lou Fran, Jim Simms, Skinny Ray Howard, Duckie McGhee. When we went to a tournament, the tournament was ours. We were the team that everybody wanted to beat. When we walked in to a tournament it seemed as if most people said, 'Give them all the trophies. Just give them all the first- and second-place trophies and we'll fight for the third-place trophies.' We were like the old Chicago Bears of 1985. They knew they were going to be whooped, the question was just how bad.

The martial artist today is more Hollywood. I was looking at a brochure the other day out at Tolo-Naa's School and it said that first prize was $1,000. I remember when we first came along, when we went to a tournament, the only thing you got was a pat on the head. There was no such thing as even a trophy. I think that the newspapers, the media, especially the movies, really perverted the martial arts. They've taken the martial arts out of the realm of what it actually is, and put it into a Hollywood setting. I've met all of the masters and the things I see portrayed as part of Karate on TV don't exist. It's just Hollywood. The students today go into the martial arts with the idea, `I'm going to become a black belt in Karate or I'm going to go out, I'm going conquer the world. I'm going to be a Bruce Lee, or a Steven Seagal,' who incidentally is an Aikidoka. Or 'I'm going to be this other guy from Europe, Jean Claude Van Damme.'

"I want to be invincible." This attitude has perverted the martial arts. It has taken the martial arts from what it is, which is basically a very spiritual thing, a very strict regimen. They perverted it with money. Kids coming in nowadays, they don't want to study Karate . All they want to do is get the recognition. In the late 1960s, we had a profusion of self-promoting black belts and that, along with certain oriental institutions that came to the United

Robert Brown (left) with student. Courtesy of Robert Brown.

States, really did some things that were not in the best interest of Karate. Karate is not as strong as it was 30 years ago when I started. When we came along, you had to be a dedicated student. Instructors back in those days would weed you out very quickly. If you weren't dedicated and you weren't really sincere about becoming not only proficient in martial arts but really living, upholding the very essence of the martial arts, you were weeded out very quickly. Nowadays, students come in, and as long as you can pay the fees, whatever they are, that's okay. The instructors will hang on to you.

I remember when I first started my training in Karate, you had to learn the basics. You had to learn how to punch properly. You had to learn how to kick properly. You had to learn how to block properly. And from there, you began to go into the study of Kata (solo prearranged fighting forms). Freestyle was not a big thing. It was an ingredient, but it wasn't important. You had to learn how to put all of your basic moves together. You had to learn to execute Kata properly. There were about 14 stances in Karate that you had to master and be able to maneuver smoothly in those stances. There were something like 50, 55 striking techniques that you had to learn. There were 25, 30 kicks that you had to master from both the left and the right side. When you started out in Karate, you learned certain basic Katas. You went through the pinans, certain low-ranked Katas, basic Katas, 12-step Katas. And you had to show proficiency in those Katas.

As you began to move on, as you began to develop, you went on to your higher ranking Katas such as your Kon Ku Sho, your Bassai Dai. The emphasis was placed on Kata, not Kumite, not fighting. You have to learn how to fight. This was a natural result of learning the basic techniques. But the study of Karate is basically the perfection of the basics. You had to learn the basics of the first forms. You have to be a very well- rounded person. I know our instructor, we had a Judoka named Gene Wyka. There were certain techniques in Judo that we had to learn, certain throws that became part of his instruction. And Aikido, there were certain techniques of Aikido that were incorporated to make you a well-rounded person. These techniques are not taught anymore in schools that I have visited since I closed mine.

I drop into new schools quite frequently. I was up in Kenosha, Wisconsin and I walked in, and I just took a look. I stayed in about one, two minutes, that's enough to make you sick, what's really taught. In Chicago schools, you name them, nobody knows me, nobody recognizes me. So you walk in and you watch and it's ridiculous, the things that are taught as being Karate .

In my martial arts students I look for dedication. You take any student who really wants to learn. You take any person who's got his mind on studying the martial arts, studying Karate, and really learned Karate in depth. If he's willing to come back and take what I put on him, I'll teach him. He's my student. And believe me, I've put some hurts on them. In our school, our students used to run three miles before workout. After running three miles, they exercised for about an hour because it's very important to be physically conditioned and then I would teach them.

A lot of people have a lot of negative things to say about John Keehan, my primary instructor. But when I look back on John, I think maybe he was a little bit ahead of his time. One of the first major martial arts tournament in the United States was given by John, at the University of Chicago, in 1963. I had a chance to meet all of the world masters of that time, and talk to them. I met Peter Alexander, Ed Parker from California, Trias from Arizona, Jhoon Rhee, even Bruce Lee was there. And of course, Bruce Lee, he looked only about sixteen, seventeen years old. He really wasn't popular like he became subsequently. But you had a chance to meet all of the masters. From that tournament you could see that John was a person who could get things done, would go out and get things done. He came to a heartbreaking end, but he was really a guy who was a go-getter and deserves a lot more credit than he was given. He held the the first Karate tournament in the United States. But before that, people practicing the different styles would not come together. 'My style is better than yours. I'm not going to compete with you.' John got them to come together and sit down and say, `Let's see who and what is actually the best.' Incidentally, he won that tournament. I think he took about 80% of the trophies at that tournament.

I was a purple belt there; Tolo-Naa had just made first degree black belt at that tournament. But the slide-in drop kicks that they do today? The first time that kick was performed, Tolo-Naa did it. There was Al Gene and Caraulia, Doug Dwyer and a bunch of guys. It was a wonderful time.

Out of the guys that I've promoted to black belt, six of them are doctors, five fellows and one lady, Sharon South, who is currently head of emergency services at County Hospital. Gregory and Stan Porter and another gentlemen, I can't remember his name. He wasn't a black belt, but he was my student and he did become a doctor. Gwendolyn Williams is a lawyer currently practicing in Denver. Bernard Brousard, was a bank vice president in Milwaukee. George "Bucky" Cole, was one of my students. He's my wife's cousin and has a position with the Red Cross. And then there was Vita. We used to call him Baker. He went on to become a member of the only black tumbling group to tour with Barnum and Bailey. He's got his own acrobatic group. He's teaching now. Bob McNutt, who was the first black belt that I produced, is the head of a data processing company in Gary, Indiana. Lethel Vaughn, also a black belt, is an over-the-road truck driver. A big, nice guy. Then there were a few who went into the ministry. Marcus Chassagne, he wasn't a black belt. Lionus McAlfin I believe was a minister and he has a church on 62nd and Vernon. He was a brown belt in the school.

My school was open from 1964 to 1970. It was on 67th and Stony Island, on the first floor. I refused to let my students lose. I refused to let my students do anything but succeed. I tried to train them not only

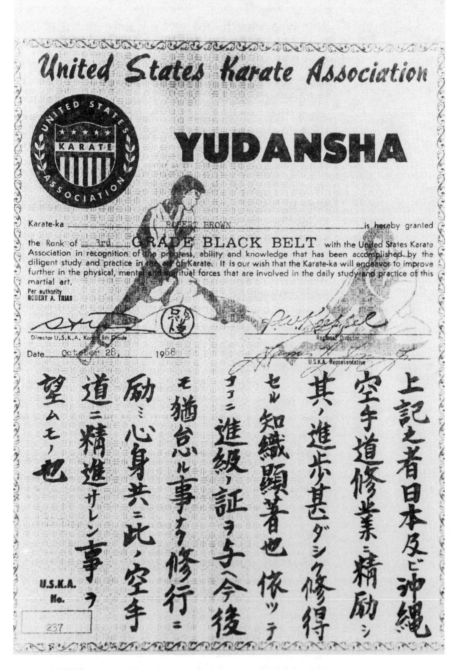

United States Karate Association

YUDANSHA

Karate-ka _____ ROBERT BROWN _____ is hereby granted

the Rank of ___ 3rd ___ GRADE BLACK BELT with the United States Karate Association in recognition of the progress, ability and knowledge that has been accomplished by the diligent study and practice in the art of Karate. It is our wish that the Karate-ka will endeavor to improve further in the physical, mental and spiritual forces that are involved in the daily study and practice of this martial art.

Per authority
ROBERT A. TRIAS

Director U.S.K.A. Korean 8th Grade

Regional Director

Date ___ October 28, ___ 1968

U.S.K.A. Representative

U.S.K.A. No.

237

上記之者日本及ビ神縄空手道修業ニ精励シ其ノ進歩甚ダシク修得セル知織顕著也依ツテ進級ノ証ヲ与ヘ今後モ猶怠ル事ナク修行ニ励ミ心身共ニ此ノ空手道ニ精進サレン事ヲ望ムモノ也

Brown's third degree black belt certificate. Courtesy of Robert Brown.

in the martial arts, but also to succeed in life. I pushed them. If my students came to me and told me, `I'm having trouble with my homework,' I'd take time to sit down and teach them. (I'm a graduate of the Illinois Institute of Technology.) I'd say, `Let's sit down and let's go over what you're having difficulty with.' I refused to let them become losers in any phase of life for any reason.

Tolo-Naa was the the greatest martial artists that I knew. I've met just about all of them. The reason I say Talo-Naa is that I've never known any person more dedicated to the martial arts. First of all, he's a world champion. I could sit here all day long and extol his virtues. He was a person that was perfection. He was a hard-driving person. Everything that he did had to be perfect physically and mentally. I don't know a person who has stuck with the martial arts under the pressures that he's had. I've seen him sometimes when there was nobody in the school but him. In spite of the pressures of trying to keep a school open, of trying to bring something to the black community, of trying to give something to our kids, Talo-Naa still worked well under these adversities. He is a man who isn't afraid to experiment. Back in the 1960s when we began contouring the black martial arts systems, he would step out and say, 'I'm black.' Long before Jesse Jackson said, 'I'm black and I'm proud,' here was a man who said, 'I'm black.' Here was a man who altered his own uniform to reflect his blackness. Here was a man who loved Chicago and dared to travel to China to perfect his techniques in Tai Chi. A man I've known since he was 15, 16, 17 years old and he has been a martial artist all this time. He is as good as any of them, as good as the best, as good as Bruce Lee or better, as good as Chuck Norris or better. He is humble. He never promoted himself in a commercial vein and he remained true to the martial arts. I could stand here for hours extolling his virtues. But I think Talo-Naa (Raymond Cooper) is the greatest martial artist that I've ever met.

I would tell a person seeking martial arts training to try to grasp the truth of Karate and the martial arts, and stick with it. Study the martial arts for the sake of studying the martial arts. Don't study with the idea of becoming a world champion or making a million dollars or going to Hollywood because this is not the trueness of the martial arts. I would tell them to push, to perfect their art, and above all, to give to other people the same as your instructor gave to you. All of the kids that came along in my school are teachers. If they're not teachers, they're dedicated in some type of humanitarian work where they're out to help our people. You see, black people right now need all the help they can get. We're the world of hurt. If we who are in positions don't stop and take the time to reach back and help two or three brothers, not for what we can get out of it, but just to give for the sake of giving, then who will? I remember a long time ago, I was shocked to find out that there were kids living right in the Robert Taylor homes (a Chicago Public Housing Project) that had never been downtown to the Loop area. Can you imagine that? Why? Because nobody's ever taken the time to reach back and say, `Hey, let's go down to the Loop,' or `Come on little brother, let's go here or let's go there.'

One of the things we never believed in was to put a student out of the school for not paying money. Many times I had to take money out of my own pocket to pay the rent on the school. I've seen Tolo-Naa over and over again take money out of his pocket to keep himself afloat. And the reason was we wanted to give to the kids, we wanted to give back something to the community, something to the youngsters coming along because these same little kids you see walking around now with the pants hanging down, funny hairdos, this is our future. You've got to work with it.

My philosophy on life is from a religious standpoint, and I'm not a religious person, spiritual but not religious. I am a very fervent follower of Jesus Christ. I believe in the Ten Commandments. I will never hurt you for any reason. My philosophy is to try to reach out and help everyone and anyone that I can and never to hurt anyone. I've read the philosophies of all the masters, and everyone else and I believe that the most important thing in life is to help someone else. To pull another brother along. Philosophy, I just live by the Ten Commandments every day.

The martial arts gave me a new direction to my life first of all. From a standpoint of personal achievments, the martial arts taught me, and this is the same philosophy I was saying, I try to give to the kids, to be a winner, to work, to let nothing defeat me. If I am defeated for any reason, not to pass the excuse on to someone else, but to recognize that my defeat was because of my own personal short comings. It has made me aware totally of me as a person, aware of both aspects, the so-called dichotomy of life, physical and spiritual. The martial arts have really taken me and shown me what I am, what I'm about. I've come to understand myself as a black man, which is very important. I realize I am not a white man, can never be a white man, will never want to be a white man. I am a black man. I've learned about my people. I've studied about my people. The martial arts have taught me to be proud of who I am and what I am. Whatever I've done in life and whatever successes I've had, I've done because of the martial arts.

I've given back everything I could to the martial arts. I've given my time, I've given my knowledge, I've given my money, as much as I could. And would you believe that in 32 years as a police officer I've never hurt another human being. I was able to go to the brothers. Some I was able to help. Some you can't help. It's impossible. Anything that was asked of me I did and I still do. One of the things we're trying to do now is really to pull a pan-African martial arts system together because we feel that this is important. This is going to have to be a must for the black martial arts in the future.

Robert Brown with members of the Chicago Judo and Karate Club. Courtesy of Robert Brown.

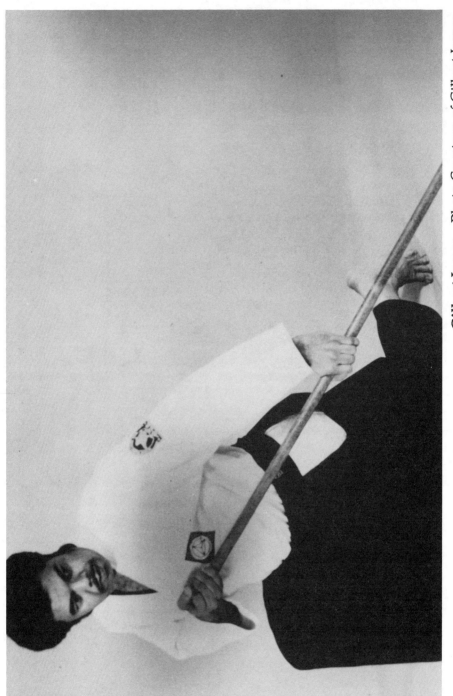

Sensei Gilbert James

Sensei Gilbert James is one of the highest ranking Aikido practitioners recognized by Japan in the United States. He is also the highest ranking black man in Aikido in the United States. James began his teaching career in 1963. He has spread the philosophy and art of Aikido throughout the Midwest.

James was born December 25, 1934, in Chicago, Illinois. His martial arts career began as a series of transitions: from Judo into Karate, from Karate into Aikido. He received a black belt in each art. As a teacher, James stressed the noncompetitive nature of the art and strove to develop his students' characters through dedication and discipline.

James is currently a staff instructor for the International Yoshinkai Aikido Federation, headquartered in Tokyo, Japan; and is the senior staff instructor for the Midwest Yoshinkai Aikido Association.

I began my martial arts training in January 1959 in Judo at the Wabash YMCA in Chicago. I was 24 years old. My instructor was Curtis Belmont. He was an instructor in Judo from the United States Marine Corps here in Chicago. He had a second degree black belt. He came and taught a few classes. He found that there were quite a few people interested so he started the formal class.

In 1961 I started Aikido training. Robert Cramer was my first Aikido Instructor at the Ju-jutsu Institute on Wabash Avenue. I continued studies in Aikido as well as Karate, Shotokan style Karate, at the Ju-jutsu Institute. Walter Nakamoto taught Shotokan. And later I trained in Karate with Sugiyama. I also studied under Bob Brown for a little while.

As I got older I felt that competition wasn't for me and I wasn't as fast as I used to be, wasn't healing quite as quickly, and I had a family, but I didn't want to give up the concepts, the philosophy of the martial arts. So I continued to study Aikido. I trained in Ju-jutsu and Kobu-jutsu, which is a form of weaponry and I also studied Kendo.

I am a second degree black belt in Judo, a second degree black belt in Karate, a third degree black belt in Ju-jutsu, a second degree black belt in Kobu-jutsu and a fifth degree black belt in Aikido. I didn't really get any rank in Kendo. I studied Kendo only about 18 months.

I had my biggest problem with Karate and I think it has a lot to do with my attitude. I'm not an aggressive individual and it showed in my Judo training too, because I didn't do that much attacking but I defended quite a bit. For some reason, I wanted to lay back and wait. Judo instructors told me that wasn't going to get it. I wasn't going to win any tournaments unless I learned how to attack. Maybe I just had a feeling against it. Karate was fine and I went through a lot of Katas, but it just didn't really give me anything.

Martial arts allowed me to gain confidence in myself and everything that I went on to do. Now I'm more aggressive, not in the physical fashion. When I go after something it's because I need to go after it. There may be some latent hold backs, or in other words, I may just reject something out of fear of failure. But martial arts has taught me how to move forward, focus forward, because I realized that we're not designed to move backwards. Our bodies aren't even made that way.

In 1963 I started teaching. I was asked to teach Judo and I wanted to try Aikido. I never ran a school, but I did teach at a number of commercial schools and colleges and universities. I've taught at DePaul, Illinois Institute of Technology (IIT), Daley College, Kennedy-King, Olive Harvey, Moraine Valley College, and St. Xavier. I taught at The Chicago Judo, Karate Centers. I taught at the park district and Martial Arts Systems. I have my own dojo in Chicago. I've had it for seven years. I don't run the place, but it's my space.

There are different styles of Aikido. There are cer-

Gilert James' Aikido Shodan certificate....Courtesy of Gilbert James.

tain individuals who think in their own way about how Aikido should be taught. And it's not incorrect. It's just that you and I are different people. We walk through that door. You step through the door with your left foot first. I may step through with my right. It's not a big question. So, I really can't say that the way I teach is different from any other person, or individual. Personalities, that's how I approach it. I teach individuals in class that way. Some of them you have to howl and scream at. And others you have to pat on the shoulder. It's called harmony.

I look for dedication and sincerity in my students. I ask them questions about why they are coming here, why they want to study with me. I analyze how dedicated they are going to be. Some say, `I'll just come in and study self-defense.' Some say to develop, to coordinate their mind along with their body, which I think is a correct answer, the best answer. That's the way I look at it because I don't teach self-defense.

Self-defense gives you linear thinking, just focusing in one area. And it takes years and years of experience to really learn techniques of self-defense. You have to have a mind for it. You have to believe that the techniques are going to work and you have to have confidence in it and yourself, confidence in the instructor who teaches it too. If you have an attitude that you're here just for self-defense, you're not going to learn the fine points of it, the intricacies of it, how to focus, or how to control your mind. You'll learn just the physical aspect of it. And that can be dangerous. You're learning just enough to get yourself killed. That's not a fact. That's just my opinion. But the techniques that I teach can be used for self-defense. We practice from the standpoint that we are being attacked. The idea is to have an open mind toward something like that if the situation comes up. You won't have to sit there and wonder, `Am I supposed to block high or block low or step here or do this,' but it's just sort of a natural movement. Your training comes into play to defend yourself. It could be just a case of talking your way out of a situation or walking

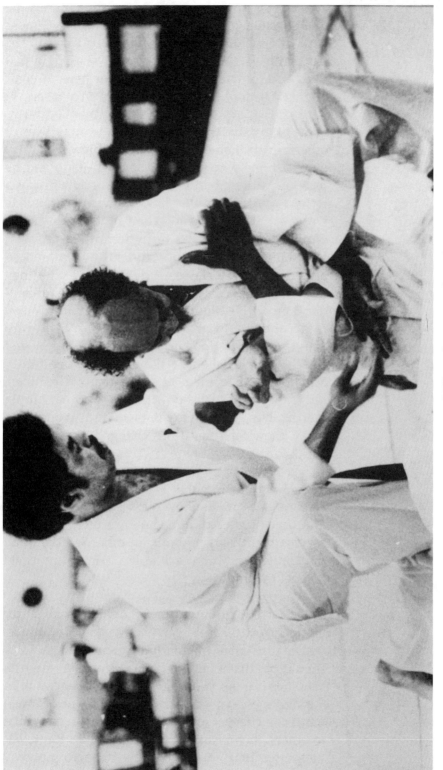

Gilbert James and students....Photo Courtesy of Gilbert James.

away or picking up a brick. Many students ask me that question 'What do you do if somebody attacks you?'. I say, 'I'll pick up a chair and do Karate.' The student says, 'You're not going to use Aikido?' I say, 'Aikido may not be the answer here. A chair might be better.' So you learn to use what's best.

Some of my students have gone on to other lives or other careers. For example, Tommy Brewer is a student of mine who's a black belt in Aikido and he recently ran for Sheriff. He's a black guy who has a lot of experience in that law enforcement area. He was an FBI agent. And when he came back, he would always find me to tighten up his control techniques. As far as other students I've influenced outside my own classes, I don't know who they might be. I'm not necessarily taking credit for anyone's growth because I think, it's up to the person to go ahead and grow because I don't develop champions. The individual's growth is not just through Aikido alone. Aikido may be one factor. Maybe it helped them to see in many directions. But if they choose to say Aikido is a primary thing in their lives, let them say it. I won't say it because I don't know for sure. It has changed my life. I can speak for me.

The great difference that I see today is really about ego and ego growth, how good I am, how bad you are, that type of thing. They are using physical aspects to try and prove it. In other words, in all the contests nowadays, it's like 'win at any cost.' Just get the trophy.

I'm involved with my students, who may be teaching incorrectly, I feel I can change that. But others, no. For instance, if this is the way you think it should be, that's the way you're going to teach it. Who am I to tell you to go to the left instead of to the right? We can sit and discuss things and if I feel that I can change your ways and/or you can listen to others, then I can contribute more. If I think that you're teaching something very dangerous, I may say something, not to change it, but to add to it.

I think in the 1960s it was a case of choosing the

Gilbert James practicing Aikido....Photo Courtesy of Gilbert James.

most popular art to be self-promoted in. Aikido is a very quiet art. There's no competition involved. There are no winners. There are no losers. You don't really have any bad attitudes. And for those type of people, if the art doesn't realize any popularity, then what's the point of being in it? You might have a master who's 30 years old. That's weird to me.

Who promotes these people? Let's say you've been studying three or four years and you made first, second degree black belt. It's authentic. But maybe you don't like the way the instructor is teaching, his philosophies, his methods, or whatever. You pull out. You take what you know and then you start adding some things to it, just redesigning it, give it a new name. No one's going to come study with you if you're just a second degree so you've got to promote yourself to sixth or seventh degree. It's like people who tell me they own their own business. You can own a paper stand and be a CEO of that company. But I don't think you can have lunch with the people from IBM and Sears and AT&T. It's the same thing in the arts. Some people cannot prove their knowledge. They're afraid. And I run across this all the time. Just listening to a person tells me where they're coming from and after that, I leave it alone. I can tell. You just pop the right words, I know you've been there. I run across a lot of that and it kind of hurts me.

I would say that the founders of the arts that I have studied would be the greatest martial artists to me, because without them I don't think I would be in them. They were Jigaro Kano, who was the founder of Judo, and Gichin Funakoshi for Karate and Moreihi Ueshiba for Aikido, and, of course, the founder of the particular system that I study now is Goza Shioda, who was a student of Ueshiba at the time. Goza Shioda was a strong energetic student. He was so rough that when the instructor said, 'Line up. Get a partner,' he'd be the last one you'd ask to train with you. The students were trying to avoid him. They knew they were in for a rough night. And he's only 5'1" and weighs about 110 pounds.

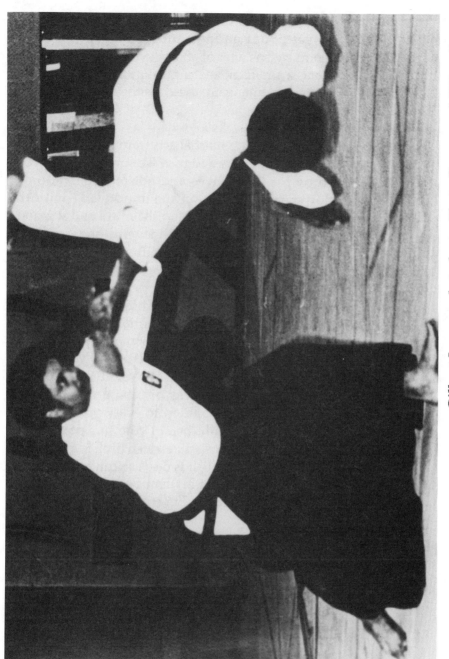

Gilbert James and student....Photo Courtesy of Gilbert James.

He's 77 years old now. He's not a ruffian. He moves about an inch and you move across the room. He has a lot of ability to anticipate the movement, a small movement, to utilize it. I look up to peers, too, but again, these are the ones I really look up to.

To those seeking martial arts training I can only tell them to be sincere and to make sure they're there to study for themselves and not for recognition or power, but to develop the mind along with the body. So often we develop the mind and we don't develop the body, or we develop the body and don't develop the mind. The first step is coming to practice.

My philosophy is to live and let live. If you can't change it, leave it alone. It's almost like the serenity prayer. If you can't change something, you don't get upset over it. It's like, if life gives you lemons, make lemonade out of it. What I've gotten out of the martial arts is a way of coping with things. I don't know life's solution to every problem, but I feel I can cope with them. Up to this point, that's what I've done. What I've given back is dedication. Aikido is part of me. It is me. You can't take it away from me. You cut off my limbs so I can't physically practice, but mentally I'm still there. Where I go, it goes.

I have two children who practice the art, two girls, I have two grandsons, 10 and 15, who practice. I don't push them. I don't necessarily want them to follow in my footsteps as far as martial arts is concerned. That's their choice. If they want to train, it's not a case of going to train with me tonight just because there's nothing good on TV. Once you start, you stay.

I'd like to see martial arts in all phases go on and I hope that the promoters don't ruin it. Fighting arts and competitions have a tendency to influence people. Say if you are a competitor and I promoted a tournament that will get you a few hundred dollars if you win, and then there's another tournament that has no rewards other than first or second

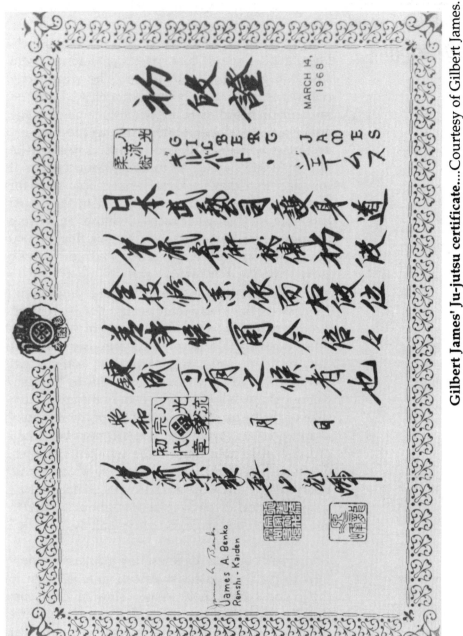

Gilbert James' Ju-jutsu certificate....Courtesy of Gilbert James.

place, maybe a dinky little ribbon, where do you think most people might go?

I hear a lot of people come back from a tournament say, `My guys got 15 trophies.' The word "trophies" keeps them in the martial arts. As I look on my bulletin board there are five tournaments going on. First place winner, $1,000. Another tournament, first place winner, $750, and so on and so on. A lot of people will sign up for that $1,000 tournament if they feel that they can win. And people train for that. Some people start training so hard to reach a level that they've never reached before. They were training at this level, maybe someone flops $1,000 down in front of them and all of a sudden they start training harder instead of just trying to improve themselves just for the sake of improving. It's easy for me to say that because I've been there. I've never been in a tournament where money was offered. In Judo, the rewards are very low, but they're there. You can get trophies, you can get medals. Karate's the same thing. But in Ju-jutsu, Kobu-jutsu, Aikido, nothing. I study the arts for the sake of the history of the arts. One of the reasons I didn't go over to the Chinese arts was because I didn't feel I could handle the two philosophies, Chinese philosophy and Japanese philosophy. Everything I did was Japanese and I can tie it all together. I don't have to worry about trying to learn another language or another culture.

I do speak courtesy Japanese for my class. I know how to thank people, ask directions. I've been to Japan and I know how to ask `How much is that item?' I didn't get too deep into Japanese culture because I realized my culture was here, not over there. I wasn't trying to make myself Japanese. If I wanted to do that, I would've moved. I had an opportunity to move to Japan. I don't think any place would be better than America.

I don't make loud noise. I don't stomp my foot very hard. It's just easier for me to do it that way. Again, what's easier for me is not necessarily easier for you. That's why we have differences in this world. It's not wrong. It's just different. Something else I tell people about in my classes, is that this or that movement is not wrong. It's just different. Because it's different, it doesn't fit what our objective is. Choose one that fits. So I tell you, that's the same way with life, so soft and easy. If it's raining outside, I can't stop it, so I take an umbrella and keep on going.

Shaha Mfundishi Maasi....Photo Courtesy of Mfundishi Maasi.

Shaha Mfundishi Maasi
(William Nichols)

Shaha Mfundishi Maasi is one of the premier researchers of black contributions in the martial arts who is still alive today. His research began back in 1966 while he was employed as a body guard for Imamu Amiri Baraka (Leroy Jones). (Editors note: Leroy Jones was a poet, playwright and community activist out of Newark, New Jersey. He was the founder of a committee which was a major political arm in electing Kenneth Gibson, Newark's first black Mayor.) Maasi embarked on a two-decade undertaking of scholarship into the origins of the martial arts and its black influence. Maasi is the co-founder of the Kupigana Ngumi African Martial Arts system.

Maasi was born October 9, 1941, in Neptune, New Jersey. His martial arts career, teaching and training, has spanned more than 33 years. He trained with several legendary martial arts instructors: Sensei James Cheatham, Grandmaster Allan Lee, and Doctor Oe Maung Gyi the "Father of American Bando."

Through Kupigana Ngumi, an eclectic African martial arts system combining traditional and contemporary martial arts principles and techniques, Maasi continues the legacy of strong martial arts training: hard practice, well-grounded principles, and the promotion of spiritual growth through the martial arts.

I began my martial arts training in 1959 in the Marine Corps. I was part of an M.P. detachment in Quonset Point, Rhode Island Naval Air Station. One of the NCUs staff sergeants trained in Karate in Okinawa and he trained in Ju-jutsu and Judo in Japan. He began a training session for those of us who were in the guard detachment. From there, I was transferred in 1960 to Kaneohe Bay, Hawaii. My platoon sergeant, Robert Hope from American Samoa, was a Kempo Karate black belt. He trained me in Kempo. In 1962 I was discharged from the Marine Corps after four years of service.

I heard about James Cheatham. In fact, a friend of mine was going to a gas station where Chea Chea worked there part-time, and Chea Chea happened to give my friend his personal card. I'll tell you how you mentally block yourself sometimes. I was tired and sleepy when the call came from my friend. I didn't want to talk to anybody. I'm tired. I was on the phone, kind of groggy. He said, 'I ran into somebody into that Karate thing, you know that thing you were doing in the service. If you want to keep it up, I got his card.' I said, 'All right, bring the card.' The next day he showed up with the card. I said, `Yeah, I'll go on down and check it out.' I walked into the school and I saw this brother sitting behind the desk. He just had a kind of energy about him. I spoke to him. He signed me up. Just his intensity brought about an intensity in me and 11 months later, I was a black belt.

He had 45 to 60 students. A good percentage were black. His first generation black belts were all white. These were people he trained back in 1956, 1957, 1958. And we came along and they just kind of drew away. They felt we cut into their territory. Chea Chea had a good name in Newark. We were the only black school in Newark, New Jersey and either you went to Dukers A.C., which was boxing or came to James Cheatham's school. He always had a good turnout.

Chea Chea didn't go into theory. I believe we have to go beyond learning by rote. We see it, we memorize it, we imitate it, but don't know what principle it's based upon. That's the only negative thing I could say about the school. It was strictly physical.

There was good physical grounding in Chea Chea's school. We were walking down the floor drilling, stop, mop up the sweat, continue. Sparring, stop, mop up the blood and sweat, and continue. I remember one night Prentiss Newton hit me and my teeth came through my bottom lip. I just covered it and we just kept dealing. I went and got stitched up afterwards. That's the kind of place it was.

I was satisfied with the physical training. And I've always been a voracious reader, so I supplied the lesson myself. Whatever he didn't tell me I'd just go over to the library and read. I read all of D.T. Suzuki's books, No Zen, Masoitan, I read all those, and Mas Oyama, and Karate by Nishiyama. I supplied what I needed on the intellectual side.

The most valuable elements I obtained from my martial arts training was knowledge of self. I learned of my limitations. I learned my fear, my needs and desires. I learned the three basic motivations for human beings. I would say really looking into my interior self, looking inside. That's what I've gotten from the art, more than the physical side. I've really come to understand and I know it to be a vehicle for enlightenment.

I was investigating dental school, working with plates and parts. The instructor wouldn't go that much into it. I lost interest and I just quit going. I decided to pursue Karate and work to support myself and that was it.

During the 1960s through 70s we fought stronger, meaning the techniques were stronger. We didn't know as much as they know nowadays. But we knew it better. I feel we knew it better because of the execution. Now I see legs flipping and that just never happened before.

What I see nowadays is they're more martially literate. They know 10 times what we knew. They can trace branches of systems. They know founders, a founder's family, that type of thing. And they're much more versed in principles of martial arts, not just learning by rote again. Not the attitude of, 'I come to class. I'm quick to learn. I'm strong. I'm in good shape. I see the kick. I practice the kick. I get better educated. I win tournaments with the kick.' But we don't understand how the kick evolved. So that's what we have now, a historical understanding about the art and how to utilize it as an instrument for evolution. Then let's fight. Kata is good, but it's mostly fighting. It's akin to a long staff, where Shuto [knife hand strike] is akin to an ax or a hatchet. We didn't see that then. Now we understand the whole weapon chain, the evolution of weapon fighting, and we can trace it back to East Africa, that type of thing.

It's not total yet, but I think there's a better understanding of how the art can be utilized as an instrument for enlightenment. Not just, say, body, mind, and spirit, but the actual path. That path for spiritual growth has been illustrated and highlighted so many times, I'd say in the last 10, 15 years. I think that's why martial artists of today are head and shoulders above us. They are more in touch with the various methods of obtaining enlightenment through the arts.

In my students I look for commitment. We all say that, but I've been accused of being fanatical about commitment. And I guess I am. It wouldn't take much for me to tell you, `Okay, your wife is working late. You're with the children. You find a babysitter, a good babysitter. You don't want to leave the child with anybody. But you make an effort to come to class because you've already missed three. I understand you have responsibilities, but if you're going to do this, you do this. If not, let's forget it. We're not going to do it partially. I'm not going to let you catch up three days after I've taught everyone else.' Many times in my relationships with people I've had that abrasive attitude.

I look for the ability to train hard, meaning to exert yourself, to learn quick, to be smart. I don't like to have to make the same correction twice because that's a waste. If you're sharp, if you belong in this class then you heard me the first time. If you're really sharp I don't have to correct you. You saw the way I placed a foot where I turned. You saw the articulation, even if you didn't know what it was, you picked it up. And later on after class, you say, 'I noticed you did so and so, why did you?' If I have to tell you for the third time, I'm not so sure you belong in the class. And I've never had financial success as a teacher. I have to do other things to make up the difference. I've never been willing to

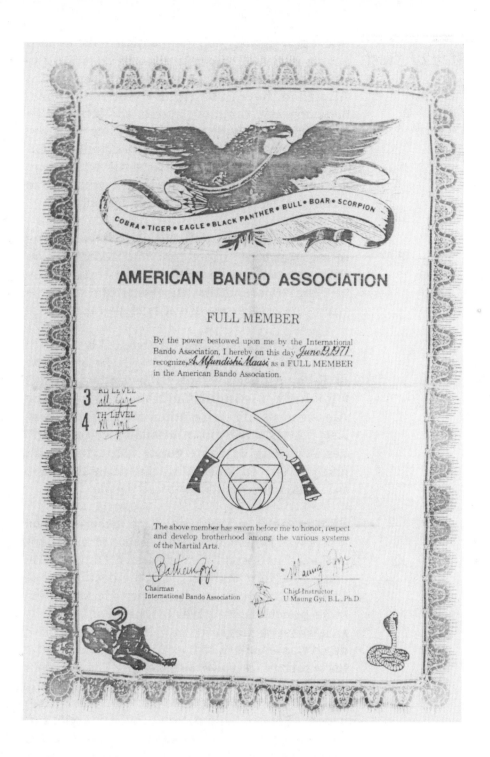

Maasi's membership certificate for the American Bando Association.
Courtesy of Mfundishi Maasi.

softstep or coddle people or be diplomatic to keep people in class. The person must be committed to train hard, willing to sweat and bleed, if necessary. And then, be a good fighter, not robot hard. Someone who can move, move, and strike as he moves. Someone who can perceive, have the sensitivity to move, to strike, constantly circling, constantly angling. So I look for a person who has an advanced kind of background, or a proclivity to matial arts, someone who has a lot of agility.

If a student comes in with two left feet, that's going to require some serious time and dedication on their part and your part, I know. And I usually suggest they find another school that can take time with them because really that's not my mission.

I influenced Mfundishi Haasan Salim. I believe I'm the second person he's trained with. He's gone on to distinguish himself highly. I have other students who have distinguished themselves in the American Bando Association. Most of my black belts have been very instrumental in the communities—working, teaching young folks. You won't find them in Black Belt Magazine or anything like that. But good, community-based people.

First, in my estimation, one of the greatest martial artists was James Cheatham, because of his contributions. The second, Grand Master Alan Lee. He helped me in many ways after the death of Chea Chea, strictly through a friendship. He taught the same principles. He never taught me a form or a kick. What he taught me in 1966 after Chea Chea's death was actually a form of Chi Gung. He called it turtle breathing. It's very subtle, soft. The influence Alan Lee had on me had to do with the esoteric aspect of the art, what root to eat if you want this to happen. Look at the sun, take this tea or you'll suffer damage, that kind of thing. And lastly, Dr. U Maung Gyi, from Burma. He founded Bando in America. He represents for me a powerful kickboxer. His record was 60 wins and three losses. He lost all three to the same man who was one of his teachers, Captain Bolin. Gyi saw action as a Gurkha. The warriors from Nepal used Gurkha that evolved from a Kopas blade, which is a kemetic knife. So he's killed on the battlefield. He's been wounded. He's been isolated on mountaintops. He's faced death many times. So to me, he represents not just a dojo master, but a true battlefield master. I think that's the next level of martial arts. You might know how to work in a dojo, you may have been good in tournaments, but there's another level of application that you need to really know if you can handle it when maybe you've been seriously wounded or injured.

Dr. U Maung Gyi took me right into the monk system, which is like Burmese Chi Gung. I was coming from such hard things to something so soft like, `Am I really there?' It kind of veered off that hard external thing. My classmates either stopped training altogether or stayed in the flavor that Chea Chea put it, whereas I went on and trained with other people. I saw the art, not just, `Can I maintain my ability to beat somebody?' as most of my classmates did. There's some other things I wanted to learn. And Gyi was very instrumental in that.

I would tell someone seeking martial arts training to know the history of the individual. The Chinese, Hebrew, Japanese. For me, Africa. You must know your history, then you can find yourself within a martial art legacy. For instance, Karate, empty hand or black hand? Kara Katash, black mongo, is known as Kara Katash, so we find the word Kara, meaning black, associated with Africans more than one place. So know your history. Then when you see yourself, you'll know yourself. When you see the Buddha, you'll know who the Buddha is. Then you'll know the conflict that the Buddha dealt with in dealing with the Hindu caste system. When you see Boddhidharma you'll know what that is. You'll know the southern Indian and the influence they had in the art, the way they influenced other Asians and the way they serve as a link between Africa and Asia.

It all has to do with knowing who you are and I keep coming back to that. For me, life is a jumping off point, a wheel. We can come back any number of times to understand what this wheel is. And when you understand it, you've gained momentum to get off of it, to free yourself of those continuous incarnations. So, for me personally, life is an opportunity to free myself of the continuous incarnations. It means to see what's going on now. What are my reactions now? What are my tendencies? What are they based on? How do they influence others? How do they conflict with what I say or what I do. So life's a total investigation. It's a testing ground. It's a battle ground. It's a meeting place. It's all of those things. I have taken from the martial arts the ability to live my life without fear or apprehension or malice. It took a while for me to get to that because I was once a very, very angry person. But I no longer have that dislike of people, incidents, or little slights. This person didn't treat me in a certain way. It's like, okay, they'll have to come back two or three times to understand that. I won't bind myself to this wheel by getting uptight about that. So, live free of fear and anxiety and anguish and malice.

I've given clarity to the martial arts. What it means to be a warrior, not mumbo jumbo. To be a warrior here and now, the way you relate to your brothers and sisters, the way that you serve your community, the way you counsel your children, the way you look after your children, the concern you have for the streets, the concern you have for school, the concern you have for the elders, the concern you have for the children being shot in driveby shootings, being raped and thrown off buildings, all that. Concern that goes beyond what's happening to me to what's happening to people.

I found the African Martial Arts Society in 1966, 1967. I was a bodyguard for Leroy Jones, and I observed his interest in African history to further identify himself with his origin. I heard him speak that time about Egypt and the contributions of the Ethiopians. It just dawned upon me that if we were here first, then we should have made some contributions that we should know about. And also, Alan Lee explained that if you really want to know the history of martial arts, you have to include

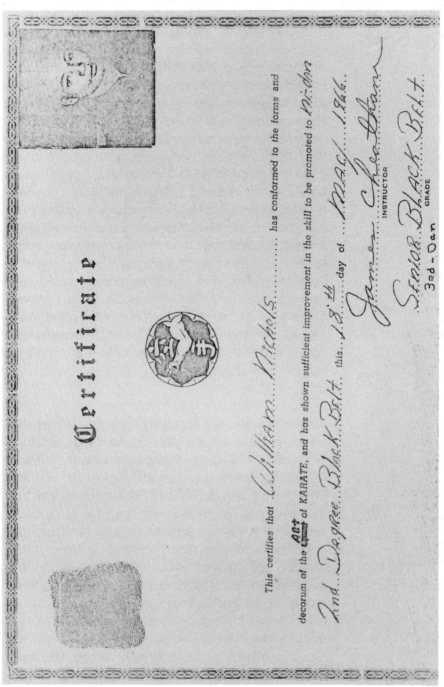

Certificate

This certifies that _William Nichols_ .... has conformed to the forms and decorum of the Art of KARATE, and has shown sufficient improvement in the skill to be promoted to _Ni-Dan_

2nd Degree Black Belt this _18'th_ day of _May_ _1966_.

James Cheatham
INSTRUCTOR

Senior Black Belt
3rd-Dan GRADE

Maasi's second degree black belt certificate in Karate. Signed by James Cheatham....Courtesy of Mfundishi Maasi.

Egypt. From Egypt to India to China to Okinawa to Japan. That's the way he explained it. So these things influenced me to begin my own investigation. Meantime, Tolo-Naa in Chicago was doing the same thing. And we hooked up through Tayari, his student, who came to the East coast. Then Tolo-Naa and I began conversing. I was using the term Ya Ngumi and I was meaning way of the fist. Ya Ngumi, Ya, meaning way of, and Ngumi, meaning fist. And he was saying Kupigana Ngumi. And I liked that term. I said, 'Brother, Kupigana Ngumi has more of a thrust than Ya Ngumi, so I'll go along with that.' From there, we began investigating principles of the art. His thing was Tai Chi based upon universal principles. And that inference had a very spiritual thing about it. We were also interested in understanding the black man's contributions through observing the heavens. Then we knew we had something to do with some of these heavenly bodies that other folks had based their thing on. And one thing led to another and over the years we came in contact with other martial artists who were interested.

I came in contact with a brother who trained with some of my students back in the 1960s, again in 1985, and he made investigations into the African origin of the art through his travels in East and West Africa. We decided to hold a conference and discuss some of these things that he discovered, some of these issues and events detected throughout human history that involved us. At the first meeting we sat with about 10 or 15 brothers and we decided we would continue our association, working in our respective communities and research and propagate African martial arts. We get that `Come on, have you been to Africa?' If you ask me, if you want to be technical, I'm an African of Jamaican parentage. I can trace my line a little more directly. I know some of my roots.

I also study through principle. I don't study through technique. I don't look at a kick and say that looks like a kick in an African dance. I study the principle. Do I find that principle very apparent in traditions in West Africa, Central Africa, East

Africa, Sudan, North Africa? How about some of
the bordering empires and communities and city-
states? What do they have that reflect the African
culture? And do I find that going deeper and deeper as I go through their territory? Also can I trace
that back to American influence? That's the way I
go about it. Understanding that Caporiera is
Central African, and Golan fighting is based upon
the movement and fighting of zebras. You see
zebras spin and kick. We can see the connection
there is based upon the movement of trees, of the
wind blowing. It's also called Ngola. It's been a
trip.

Nganga Mfundishi Tolo-Naa.....Photo Courtesy of Mfundishi Tolo-Naa.

Nganga Mfundishi Tolo-Naa
(Ray "The Chicago Tiger" Cooper)

As a young Karate tournament fighter in the early 60's, Tolo-Naa beat one of the legendary Shimabuku brothers and lost a controversial decision to Mike Stone, an undefeated Karate champion. He was widely respected as an innovative young fighter and teacher of Karate, having studied under the infamous Count Dante.

Mfundishi Tolo-Naa was born Raymond Cooper on January 1, 1946 in Chicago. After he left Karate he later turned to the internal Chinese arts and mastered Tai Chi Ch'uan, Hsing Yi Ch'uan and Pa Kua Ch'uan. As an instructor Tolo-Naa emphasizes the idea of perfecting the mind, body, spirit, and technique. He learned of Taoist principles (maintaining balance, going with the flow) when he was 12 years old and these principles continue to influence him today.

Tolo-Naa is a man of his convictions. He received a dishonorable discharge from the United States Army after serving eighteen months imprisonment for refusing to fight in Vietnam.

He is widely respected and recognized as a teacher and co-founder of the Kupigana Ngumi African Martial Arts System. He is one of the premier researchers of African influences in the martial arts today.

I began my martial arts training at about 12 years of age with my brother, who had been discharged from the Army as a ranger. He was studying some martial arts at the time and started as soon as he was discharged. So I started Karate and a lot of discipline exercises, push-ups, sit-ups. He was extremely rough on me. He was probably about 28 then.

When I began studying Karate there was very little, if any, material on Karate. There was only one martial arts periodical, that was "Judo Digest". And interestingly enough, one of the instructors who appeared monthly was a black martial artist named Master James Cheatham. He was teaching Karate at the time. He was out of Jersey. In those days he was traveling abroad, Hong Kong, Japan, Okinawa, various stops. I used to buy the magazine, began to learn techniques, and try to find as much as I could on Karate . There were hardly any books, those days, you're talking about 1958-1959.

Later I enrolled formally with John Keehan in 1963. He was in Chicago. I was about 17 years old when I first visited the dojo with a friend, James Sims. There was a tournament going on, a small, indoor school tournament. I had told Mr. Keehan that I had some training, I had been training on my own for about four years. He asked me if I would like to spar in the tournament, so I did. I started at white belt rank, and I beat all of his white belts. He put me in the colored rank. I beat his colored rank up through purple. He put me in brown belt. I beat all his brown belts. He didn't want to put me in a black belt. He was afraid I might embarrass his black belts. So he asked me to accept some rank, blue belt. And shortly after that he moved his dojo to 79th and Ashland. That was the year of the first world Karate tournament at the University of Chicago field house. And that year, I made brown belt. And I placed third, tied third, for the brown belt form. What happened was that a short time after that I began to take on classes. I used to teach most of his classes. That same year Jimmie Jones joined the class. And Bob Brown was there. At the same time, I was also conducting a class in Chicago Heights at a local community center. Some of the martial artists in Chicago would come to my class during the week days. I taught on the South Side on the weekend.

I attribute the most valuable part of the training to my brother. He set the ground rules. Had it not been for him really pushing me, I could have easily gone astray, not exercising and really being in shape. He would train me religiously so many pushups, situps, and chinups, running every day, skipping rope and the whole thing. He started me in my first iron palm training. He emphasized that which was very practical. I had no formal work at that time. It wasn't until I started with Keehan that

I started to learn Shorei-Goju forms.

I've had numerous schools in the South suburbs, Chicago Heights, Rock Forest, Harvey, about seven or eight in Chicago. From 1964 to the present there have been, close to a dozen schools, that's taking in all parts of the suburbs.

I think my approach in terms of the internal arts was always there. Fortunately, before I started training formally in Karate, I had the opportunity to read books on the internal system. There were a couple of books that were privately published out of San Francisco. One was entitled. "The Iron Palm Training" and one was called, "The Poison Hand Training." This was put out by the Chinatown community in San Francisco. I was lucky to run across them in a classified ad publicized by the Popular Science Magazine. The book included various philosophies, how to construct training equipment, that type of thing. I constructed such equipment in my parent's attic. About a year later, another two volume set came out of Chinatown on the Southern Style of Shaolin. So I think I approached Karate with a pretty good internal understanding. I think that's why I was able to pretty much move through the rank pretty fast and be able to train a lot of people at that time.

Fortunately, and unfortunately, I was introduced to the racism in martial arts at an early age which caused me to pretty much seclude myself. In 1964 I competed in the Jhoon Rhee Nationals in Washington, D.C. It was probably one of the biggest tournaments in the United States at that time. It was very well organized. It brought in competitors from all over the world. That same year I just made my first degree black belt, probably about a month before the tournament. As you know, traditionally, when you match competitors up, you try to do it by rank, and you gradually build up until you finally come to the higher ranks. It appeared that everybody was ranked according to the various levels. The guest of honor at that particular tournament was Shimabaku, a very famous master out of Okinawa a sixth degree black belt. He was there to compete. So, because I was a new black belt and a black man, they figured they'd throw me in for him to fight first, to make it look more impressive on his part. Unfortunately, I beat him in his first match. And that's when I got my first look at racism because all the corner judges and the center referee, who happened to be Ed Parker, [Editors note: Ed Parker founded the first commercial Karate school on the West Coast in 1954.] just couldn't believe it. They refused to give me the points.

With Shimabuku, the corner judges actually got up and took their chairs and threw them, said it wasn't supposed to be. They refused to give me the points I scored. Even upon appeal. And it wasn't until Jhoon Rhee [Editors note: The Father of Taekwondo in America.] intervened that I won the match. And then in the latter part of the year, in September, when I competed in world competition the same thing happened with Mike Stone and Trias was the center referee, we went through the same scenario. There really wasn't any competition. So it was bad having to deal with the politics of racism, but it was good because it caused me to be more focused and begin to seek out the African origin of the martial arts and try to organize black martial arts.

I think there is definitely a difference between the martial artists of yesterday and the martial artists of today. I think what happened is a lot of people who termed themselves martial artists are really not martial artists. They tend to think that because they practice in the dojo, wear a black belt around their waist, read the magazines, and go to the tournaments that they call themselves martial artists.

It seems like that whole cycle is colored by just the politics, just the commercialism. Very few martial artists get into the spiritual side of the art. In ancient times a martial artist and his training had to reflect not how good he was, but how he carried that over into his family, into his community, and finally to the nation. It's not a white/black thing to see problems of gangs, the violence, the drugs. But

UNITED STATES KARATE ASSOCIATION

ARIZONA
ALASKA
CALIFORNIA
COLORADO
CONNECTICUT
ENGLAND
FLORIDA
GEORGIA
HAWAII
ILLINOIS
INDIANA
IOWA
JAPAN
KANSAS
KOREA
LOUISIANA
MAINE
MASSACHUSETTS
MEXICO
MINNESOTA
MISSOURI

NEBRASKA
NEW JERSEY
NEW YORK
NEW MEXICO
NEW HAMPSHIRE
NORTH CAROLINA
OHIO
OKINAWA
OKLAHOMA
OREGON
PENNSYLVANIA
PHILIPPINE IS.
PUERTO RICO
SOUTH AFRICA
SOUTH DAKOTA
TENNESSEE
TEXAS
UTAH
WEST VIRGINIA
WISCONSIN

CERTIFICATE

Karate-ka _RAYMOND LEE COOPER_ is hereby granted the rank of _1st DEGREE BLACK - SHO-DAN_ with the United States Karate Association in recognition of the progress, ability and knowledge that has been accomplished by the diligent study and practice in the Okinawa-Japanese origin art of Karate. It is our wish that the Karate-ka will endeavor to improve further in the physical, mental and spiritual forces that are involved in the daily study and practice of this martial art.

望ムモ也 道二精進サレン事ヲ 励ミ心身共二此ノ空手 モ猶台ル事ナク修行二 ヨヨニ進級ノ証ヲ与ヘ今後 セル知識顕著也 依ッテ 其ノ進歩其甚グシク修得 空手道修業二精励シ 上記之者日本及ビ沖縄

Per Authority of U.S.K.A.
Director Robert A. Trias

Date _Feb 3rd_ _1964_ U.S.K.A. No _229_

Tolo-Naa's first degree black belt certificate....Courtesy of Tolo-Naa.

we don't see the martial artist today trying to really make a difference in dealing with it head on.

Just like I tell my students all the time, years ago when the Kung Fu movies first came on the scene, what you had is a lot of people who reviewed movies. All they saw was really stylists. This was Mantis, this was Shaolin, this was Tiger-Crane. Everybody viewed the various styles and how flashy the practitioner looked. But rarely did they understand the whole theme or the plot of the story. It was always somebody fighting against injustice. It was always fight between right and wrong. Right always came out on top. So the Chinese put a very good story out in terms of the practitioner always using his skills to fight injustice. We just don't see that nowadays.

During the 1960s people were beginning to come into black consciousness. You found what happened was that various groups emerged like the Black Panther Party, S Group, Snick, Core and various groups. You find a lot of martial artists at that time starting to branch off and get into various groups to fight discrimination, things that were going on in the South, all over the United States. You find a lot of people who were very active at that time, particularly James Cheatham. He was very vocal at that time. He was a Muslim. He was with Elijah Mohammed out of his mosque in New Jersey. He died in a plane crash, I think that was around 1965 or 1966. He was so ahead of his time. He was taking students to China, all over the world. After seeing him in a magazine in 1963, Bob Brown, Jim Sims and I went to the Toronto National Championship. I got a chance to meet him at that time. He brought in a group of Karate students from New York, New Jersey area. They completely dominated the whole tournament. There was no competition whatsoever. They were that disciplined, that rough.

I emphasized good basics. A lot of time is spent on stances, good leg work, just being in good physical shape. There's a saying that in China a person could spend as many as two years on stances.

Mfundishi Tolo-Naa and students....Photo Courtesy of Mfundishi Tolo-Naa.

Nowadays you're lucky to get two months in on stances. So we spend a good six months on foundation work and understanding the principle. I think the idea of the principle, as well as technique are important. Whatever I have to offer, I really want to share with everyone.

Unfortunately, a lot of the information is mostly on the spiritual side. Most people don't want it, so they tend to weed themselves out. Deep down you would like to see more people take advantage of certain techniques, certain principles, information. Unfortunately, a lot of people just get locked in. They probably would never see some of the higher principles. You need to understand that the martial artists came out of very spiritual settings. In the Shaolin Monastery, they were always around the monks and the nuns and the practice. And it was mainly for staying in shape and protecting their country and fighting against injustice. The key thing was spiritual cultivation.

Nowadays we just don't have that. We have some of the ceremony with the bow of hands. It never gets really beyond that. Very few dojos even practice meditation. It's like just going through the motions. Getting in touch with the spiritual side is the most important thing. That's what makes the martial arts alive. I've seen so many martial artists reach a peak at around third degree black belt and fifth degree black belt and it gets boring to them. They end up dropping out. They get out of shape. That's because they can't understand the higher principles. They look at it just as a physical art, and don't see the spiritual side.

If you are seeking martial arts training I advise you to find a good instructor. A lot weighs heavily on the student because of media, movies, TV, and videos. They approach a martial arts school thinking it should be what they see in the movies. So right away, you find people who walk into your dojo have certain expectations and the instructor doesn't meet that and they think, `Well, that's not for me.' So it can be a very sensitive situation between an instructor and a possible student trying to get him to understand what you really have to offer. Instructors like myself aren't trying to impress anybody. Whereas at some schools, you walk in and you have the whole sales pitch and they'll try to impress you with the techniques, the various kicks and the apparatus just to put you into a contract. Too many people fall into that and really that's what they're looking for. So as a result, the martial arts really have deteriorated and become very difficult, it's almost impossible to find really good instructors.

When students come to me, I actually try to discourage them. I want to see if they really want to learn. Often they come with a preconceived idea. They studied a little bit of this or saw this in a movie. I just don't want to hear that. They figure they can sign an application, pay their money, they can demand certain things. It's not going to be. It's a master-disciple relationship. So how do you get that across in a Western culture? It's not part of our culture. People just don't understand. You can't fault the student because he has no idea. Very rarely do you find a student who comes in who has some idea of what that relationship should be. And in ancient times, I shouldn't say ancient times, even in today's China, you just don't find martial arts schools. You find a good teacher and you go to his home and you pay certain respects. You go through a trial period. He'll either accept you as a student or reject you. You go to his home to learn, work out in his back yard or a park or the countryside. So right away you eliminate the problems of the overhead of a school, paying rent, that kind of thing.

One of my best, sharpest students who really understood the spiritual side, unfortunately went through his last rites of passage about two months ago. At age 50 he died of a heart attack, complicated by lung cancer. His name was Ray Howard. A lot of people know him, in the 1960s he was very competitive. Since then I have never seen anyone kick like him. Unbelievable kicks. And he was a very spiritual person, very quiet. He had the true warrior spirit. He really took it to heart. I say that because he and I lived together with another student Douglas McGhee. We traveled a lot, we trained religiously, 24 hours a day.

Mfundishi Tayari Casel was a very good student. He's probably the most active now because he's really pushing the African traditions. Melenga Kijuana Vita was another, and, brother Kwaku who died a few years ago. And I would like to think I've touched a lot of people. A lot of people come to class, work out for some time, but you never really take them on as students. Probably the correct word is disciple, just a few of them. But a lot of people have gone to this school, hundreds and hundreds. Another one of my students right now is Aaron Hardy. He's a very good student, unbelievable.

I pretty much take what might be termed a Taoist approach of just trying to live in harmony with nature. To give you an example, when I was 12 years old I used to read an awful lot. I went to the library, which was about a mile from my home. And I remember taking a small book off the shelf and it was called, "The Tao Te Ching," which is a classic of Taoism. And it was so fascinating. When I checked this book out, I walked from the library to my home, in the summer, down the street reading this book. By the time I got home I had read the book because it's not a very long book. But it changed my life ever since because it just talked about the balance, about being in harmony with nature. It talked about taking the middle path.

My approach has been the same since that point and I think it's flowed over into my practice and the way I teach. I'm beginning to seek understanding in terms of African spirituality. The Taoism, the traditional African approach, I find that it's just the same. There's the understanding that we have teachers, we have deceased teachers, and members of our family, who are our ancestors. We owe something to them because if it hadn't been for them, we wouldn't be here. So the saying in Africa is, "I am because you are." That's very important. That idea as opposed to the thinking in the West, which is, "I think, therefore I am." It's not about that. Just try-

Tolo-Naa's student Tayari Casel...Photo Courtesy of James Jones.

ing to stay balanced, that's important.

In my entire youth, it's as though I was born to be a martial artist. I remember my mother showing me a picture of myself. I was about 8 months old. I was sitting there with a bald head, very stern look on my face, my fists clenched like this and it's been a part of me ever since. I couldn't even envision being, doing anything else but the martial arts. The only problem now is I don't have the time to devote to it. I should say I don't take the time to practice as much as I would like to.

With my teacher, Professor Huo Chi Kwang, who's still alive, 86 years old, I began the study of Tai Chi Ch'uan. I began studying with him in 1968 and we've maintained a very good teacher-disciple relationship over the years. I've since learned the Tai Chi Ch'uan and the Pa Kua. It's been a very good relationship, even the calligraphy, a lot about the Chinese mind, the oriental culture. The first thing he told me when I came to him to learn Tai Chi is that what I should remember is that the body has limitations. It can get tired or it requires rest. But the mind never needs rest. It's going on 24 hours a day, even while you sleep. So he emphasized training the mind was the most important thing. Once the mind was trained properly, that's when you don't need things like the warm-ups. You make yourself do certain things. The mind leads the body. Too often we think like this: big muscles, what have you. It's really the sayings of the mind. Chi comes from the mind and directs it. The eyes project it to whatever point you want.

My meeting Hou Chi Kwang was destiny. The Dragons Inn, a famous Chinese restaurant had just opened in Homewood. I stopped by to buy some carry out food. On the counter were some pictures of some children doing some martial arts. One girl was doing her Tai Chi Sword, matching sets. So I asked the owner who they were and who taught them. She said, `A very famous teacher, Hou Chi Kwang.' She was very excited because she said she saw him perform and do some things that were almost miraculous. She saw him walk up in a

Mfundishi Tolo-Naa with Master Lu Hung Ming...Photo Courtesy of Mfundishi Tolo-Naa.

demonstration to a guy who was about 250 pounds and stood four feet from him and took his Chi [inner energy] and knocked him down. And then Hou Chi Kwang stood on top of him, above him and started to bounce him on the floor like a basketball.

I had my doubts. But when I found out this woman was a physicist and her husband was an M.D., I asked could I meet this person. So they gave me his phone number and I phoned him. He told me to come over, and I went by, the old traditional way. He invited me in. We drank tea. I was smart enough not to say anything until he spoke. That was my first test. We drank tea for probably an hour before he finally said anything. We got up and he showed me some of his paintings and he asked me why I wanted to learn Tai Chi Ch'uan. I just told him I was curious and that's when he told me the first thing about the mind and not ever needing the rest and always keeping the mind in order. Keep it active. Shortly after, I took one of his classes and I've been with him ever since.

Mfundishi Tolo-Naa (right) with K. Vita...Photo Courtesy of Mfundishi Tolo-Naa.

James Field with students...Photo Courtesy of James Field.

Sensei James Field

For more than two decades James Field has taught Karate throughout Southern California. Field is one of the few Americans and one of the first blacks to graduate from the prestigious Japan Karate Association (JKA) instructors' course. He is presently the JKA's chief instructor for his region, and often travels internationally teaching and testing JKA affiliates.

James Field was born on October 13, 1939 in Sandy Bay, Jamaica, and at the age of 7 relocated to southern California. Field served in the United States Marine Corps from 1958 until 1961. During his tour of duty he was a member of a unit called Force Reconn which was sent to Cambodia, Indochina. Upon Field's return to civilian life, he aspired to become a professional football player with the San Diego Chargers as a defensive corner back. Although he was carried on the Chargers' roster for one year, a knee injury kept him on the side-lines. This knee injury led to his study of Karate. And thirty years later James Field has distinguished himself as one of the foremost traditional Karate instructors active in the United States.

I began my martial arts training about two years after I got out of the service. I started Shotokan Karate in 1963. I was trying out to be a professional football player. I had tried out for the San Diego Chargers. It's sort of a complicated story how I got started. My very first instructor was my brother-in-law. His name was Archie Strong. I started training, just messing around with him because of a knee injury. That was my introduction to martial arts. I seriously started training in martial arts in 1964 with Mr. Nishiyama.

The person who was most significant to me, remaining and elevating me to the level I am was Yutaka Yaguchi. He came in 1965 and I've been with him since then. There was a big difference in training with Mr. Nishiyama and Mr. Yutaka. Mr. Nishiyama didn't ignore you but he paid attention to specific people that he liked, I believe. Yaguchi was a person who just talked Karate, and if there was something that you needed, he would help you with it. I feel as though everybody got special attention from Mr. Yaguchi.

The first thing that I learned from martial arts was patience. I was told I was a very, very aggressive individual as I was growing up. I learned to channel my agression into other things. I learned to listen to other people to hear where their problem was and realize there were many times when I was the person who was not quite right in the situation. I learned about myself.

There were times I thought about quitting. That was the time right before Mr. Yaguchi arrived because as I said, the chemistry between myself and Mr. Nishiyama didn't quite blend.

I have a Santa Monica dojo. We have clubs at the universities around here and I've taught at them. I'm presently the chief instructor at the University of California-Los Angeles. I've taught Karate classes at Pepperdine University, USC,and at Loyola Merimont. I coached the Cal State Los Angeles team to a championship in 1969. We have many dojos in the region maybe 30 to 40 different dojos in my area.

I went through the Japan Karate Association's Instructor course in 1970-72 or 1971-73, I'm not real sure. That was sort of a hard time and a blur. It's very hard and to me it took more mental endurance than physical. There were times when I didn't remember (I wasn't crazy) but I just couldn't remember what day it was or what time it was or anything like that because I was so into trying to get it right.

I was one of the first black men to go through the course. I may have been the first. Yaguchi, as my instructor, had prepared me for what was to come. He had explained to me that it was very, very difficult, very hard. So I was prepared mentally and physically, working with him one-on-one for hours every day for about a year, year-and-a-half. He prepped me for it. I had an idea of what was to come.

The only other organization that I would say that the Japan Karate Association comes close to is the Marine Corps. I was in the Marine Corps. It's an organization that's well organized and it has a structure just like old Japan and that's how the Marine Corps is.

It was a very easy transition. I learned about myself. That was the major reason why I stayed in Shotokan. I had friends who trained in Tae Kwon Do and many other different styles. To me, their dojos were very undisciplined. The standards weren't there, I won't mention any names. A well-known person in the martial arts, you can go any-where in the world and you ask about this man. Everybody says, 'This man is great. He's one of the greatest martial artists. He's Asian. He told me that, 'If you come with me, I'll make you a black belt.' At that time, I was I think probably fifth Kyu [class]. He said, 'I'll make you first degree black belt and in one year you'll become second degree.' And I was FIFTH KYU and I was thinking about it and at first I thought, 'Whoa, man, black belt.' But then I thought about it. Here I am struggling with fifth Kyu and he's going to make me a black belt? That's one of the major reasons why I never changed in anything because the discipline, the standards were so, so different. The JKA standards are very, very high.

We always trained at very good basics and the training itself was rigorous and I do mean rigorous. Sensei would go through each class, no matter what the length. When you first started, the classes were two hours usually. He would start out the first hour, just white belt, beginner, basic punching, basic this, basic that and then you would go on. You would graduate from one movement to two, then to combinations, always. And I think this is what really made me strong in certain ways because we did the whole routine over and over. It wasn't like when you get to a certain level, we don't do this anymore and now we do this, like many dojos I've noticed. We just did from white belt to black belt, always. You have strength in, I call it complete range of motion, complete range of technique, and so it makes your body much stronger.

I do the same thing today. Sensei would say this is very traditional. This is the way they trained traditionally and that's all I do, also. Sensei would always keep your mind working. He would always give you these situations of life and death, feeling. I think your mind or you can call it spirit, attitude, has so much to do with the development of your technique. You can get people who can hit hard and that's not it. But if a person can hit and the attitude is penetrating, going completely through the target, there is a completely different feeling. For example, in demonstrations, Yaguchi Sensei would stand there and have you flex and make a tight stomach and he'd hit you real hard. He would ask you how it felt and you would say, 'It hurts.' Then he would hit you a second time and you would still feel a hurt in front, but your BACK, there would be this burning sensation in your back. This is the kind of thing he always emphasized when training. This is the feeling when punching. This is the attitude when you do your technique.

I really think there is a difference. The difference is, when I was training, Sensei taught us Budo [way of the warrior], like life and death. Those are the things Mr. Yaguchi would always express when we were training, feeling life and death. Now I can't get this point across to most people. They're not interested in that. A lot of people just do it for recreation, competition. The average person who comes to this dojo or who asks me about training, the first thing he does is to ask about scoring and competition. When I first started training that was the furthest thing from my mind. I didn't even want to do it.

I think training back then was much harder, much tougher, more rigorous. Very, very different in that way. We would train for hours. There were times when we would do one technique for an hour-and-

JAMES FIELD

James Field's Karate Shodan certificate...Courtesy of James Field.

a-half or two hours, however long the class was. UCLA was two hours. We would train for two hours and do probably one technique, sometimes two. Now when you teach, if you don't have a variety or a special way of teaching this one thing you want to teach, people get bored and they'll tell you about it. 'Oh, God, can't we do anything better than this? I came last week we did this and I figured we were going to do this for the rest of the week, so I didn't show up.' Karate is not as serious to them as it was to me or to us in, I always call it, the prehistoric days. The spirit, the attitude is different. I really can't come up with why that is. I haven't really thought about it that much.

When I first started training, I had a very severe knee injury. When I first started doing it, I was just doing it for that. Then I realized there was something totally different about this. In order to do this you have to put your heart and soul into it. And so my goal became to be the best you can be, but the point was to be able to execute just one technique well. I wanted to be able to do one thing where Sensei didn't say this is not right. I was looking for that perfection of technique. Working towards that I learned so much about myself and then I realized that I was training to perfect my self, my own mind, my own body and that is basically what I am still training for today. To become the best that I can be. I look for that attitude in other people. This is one of the things that I do a lot when people start training. I look at them, the way they train, their attitude, and I'm searching for that one individual. It's a long, hard search.

Here in Santa Monica I belong to an organization called PAL (the Police Activities League), and I work with a lot of children because of my own background. I have changed the lives of, not a great amount, but some youngsters who were going the wrong way. I've changed two in particular who came to train with me. One, Dan Cook, just left for Japan and he'll be there for a year. Another one was Justine Lavow. Her mother told me that she was way out there. She now has a Master's or PH.D. in marine biology. I think I've heavily influenced many of the children in the area. Many of them don't become as successful as these two people, but they do turn their lives around and that's what I want and what I like.

Yutaka Yaguchi is the greatest martial artist I ever seen, because first, he is my instructor. I've been to Japan, I've seen the new instructors and I've seen the older instructors and this man is so, so incredible. He moves like a cat. He's probably 60 years old now. The first time I saw him I was impressed because at that time, I've forgotten what rank I was, but my attitude was, 'I'm a professional football player and I can deal with anything that anyone has.' And when I saw him just moving around on the floor, it changed my mind. I never even engaged in any Kumite with him or anything. I just saw him moving and I thought, 'My God, look at this guy.' I was really impressed. In the beginning, he just treated everybody the same, and then one day, he just started. I thought he was picking at me. `What is this guy's problem?' And my roommate, who was a Japanese person, told me, 'No, no, no, he's not picking at you. He LIKES you, there's something about YOU that he likes.' I said, `Oh, man, I don't want anybody to like me like that.'

Another person who impressed me was Master Nakayama. He passed away already, I think in 1987. But when I was an instructor trainee I went to Japan to train. I went to Japan twice a year for two years and I would stay two months each time. I would train with Master Nakayama. He was probably in his 70s at that time. To watch him, it was totally amazing. He would demonstrate a punch or kick, or shifting, never combination techniques, or never complete Kata. I was very impressed. I've said this to my students many times. He had the fastest reverse punch I've ever seen in my entire life. I was so, so, so impressed and I wished that I could have seen him when he was much younger. My Sensei did, and my Sensei used to tell me about him. Since I was Master Yaguchi's student, he took time out and gave me personal instruction every now and then. He would talk to me and explain things to me. But I think he would do this with anyone.

For a person who's going to train in the martial arts, first find a good traditional instructor. To me, martial arts is not competition. Now Karate is more sports oriented. They call it the martial art. When you change and put the sports aspect into it, it's not martial arts anymore. I would suggest that they go around and look at different training and ask other people who are into Karate or the martial arts. Ask them about the martial arts. Ask them if they like or dislike competition. To me that's the important point. Flat out—what kind of dojo are you going to and what kind of structure do you have? When I say kind of instructor, that covers a lot of bases. A good martial arts instructor, to me, is a very traditional, strict individual. When I say strict, I mean he has total control over what's going on in the dojo. There have been places where I've gone to, for example when I was growing up with Karate. I would go with my friends sometimes to their dojo. And two guys would get into whaling on each other and the instructor would say something like, 'You know you guys shouldn't be doing that' or 'Get 'em men, get 'em.' That's not an instructor. An instructor has total control. When my students practice Kumite [sparring] and when I say, 'No contact,' we can spar for five hours and there will be no contact. No one in this dojo does any kind of Kumite while I'm not here. No one will do it unless I'm here. The instructor has control of what happens in that dojo. I've gone to places where everybody spars and everybody just does what they want to do. I say, 'What does your Sensei say about it?' and they say, 'Oh, well, we can just do whatever we want to do because...' It's the same at my Sensei's dojo. If he says, 'No sparring,' nobody does Kumite at all.

As far as giving back, from what I've gained from it, I don't think that I could ever give back what I've gotten from the martial arts because the people who were interested in me put so much of their lives into me to bring me to the point where I am today. And I don't think that I could ever replace that. I've gotten a real good understanding of life.

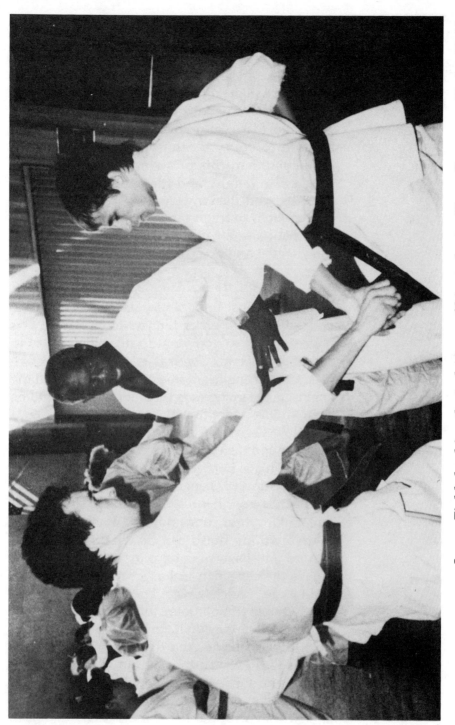

James Field checking the technique of his students...Photo Courtesy of James Field.

I've just sort of grown up. I have almost become the person I wanted to be and I never knew it. It changed me. I was a very aggressive person. I thought that there was this one thing that I wanted to do in life. It taught me, it showed me what I really wanted to do and it changed me from what I was going to be. One of the things I want to do is to be able to continue the martial arts. Master Funakoshi had this one idea in mind to teach Karate. He taught, and then Master Nakayama after him and then my Sensei. Then my idea, my goal in life is to try to carry on or teach Karate the way that I was taught by my instructor and try to carry on the traditions of Master Funakoshi, if possible.

To me, the most important person in your life is yourself. And in order for you to be happy, you have to do what you want to do. When I was in college, I was told, 'The way to go is to be an engineer. Oh, the engineers are going to get this and the engineers are going to get that and it's going to be great. You're going to make so much money.' So, I went to college and started studying to become an engineer and then about two years into it I thought it over. This is not what I wanted. I'm not happy doing this. And I changed. Actually, I dropped out for a while and then I went back to school and I was talking to a counselor and I asked him, 'Is there anything that I can do where you just go around and have fun and play games?' He said, 'That's the recreation major.' I said, 'That's what I want to do.' Basically what I'm getting at is that so many people end up doing things they really don't want to do but they do it. To me, they do it to keep up with the Joneses. And that is not my style. My style is to do what I feel and do what makes me happy. And this is what I would suggest for other people. What makes me happy is to teach Karate and to watch people progress, see how people's lives change. I have a lot of students come to me so much and talk to me. I work with the PALS and I'm always talking with the little children.

Right now I'm Rokudan [6th degree black belt]. I'm in ISKF [International Shotakan Karate Federation].

The JKA in this country is a representative of the ISKF. This ISKF sponsors me to go all over the world to teach and to test. I go every place. I've been to Central America, South America, Europe, Asia. There are many places where you become a black belt or you become a self-proclaimed instructor and you can go other places and you can test other people. But it's only recognized by you and your friend. But when I'm sent somewhere by the ISKF/JKA, if I test someone, they can go to Japan JKA and these people are recognized as that rank. That's the thing like I said about the Marine Corps where you make sergeant or corporal or whatever in a certain area. In the Marine Corps, if you make rank, they can transfer you from San Diego to Okinawa. You still have that rank and it's recognized no matter where you go in the world.

Students do situps under the watchful eye of James Jones, Jr.
Photo Courtesy of James Jones, Jr.

Sensei James Jones, Jr.

*James (Jimmie) Jones, a martial arts innovator, was born
in Mississippi on June 10, 1940. Jones was labeled the
"Sugar Ray" of Karate during the mid and late 1960s,
and he was often times referred to as "The Father of
Karate in the Midwest." He dominated the Midwestern
martial arts scene with numerous firsts: he was one of
the first Karate instructors in Chicago to attempt to
teach people of every income level, he was the first to
organize the YMCA's Karate programs in Illinois and
Indiana, and he was also the first black to serve as the
Illinois Director for the United States Karate
Association. James Jones developed the Universal Karate
System (UKS) in late 1974. He is still active in the Midwestern martial arts community by the way of lectures
and seminars.*

My martial arts training began in September of
1961, when I went to see the first world's Karate
championship at the University of Chicago. A
friend and I decided to go and both of us joined
Chicago Judo and Karate Center the day after the
tournament.

I was working at S&C Electric Company, where I
had started working since I was 18. I've been there
ever since for 34 years now. I started off as a custo-
dial worker at the very bottom of the pile. I'm a
personnel manager at S&C now.

My first instructor was John Keehan. I had always
worked under John Keehan, who was an excellent
instructor. He taught excellent fundamentals and
that's what I think is the most important criteria for
an excellent martial artist.

I earned my black belt in 13 months and I really did
not feel that I was adequately prepared as a black
belt because I had missed several of the promotions. I was still a white belt and so I was going up
at the same time as some of the brown belts. I happened to perform better than those brown belts and
so I got promoted to third class brown belt. And
then I went from brown to black because I won

mostly all of the tournaments that were given that year. I won Midwest, All-Chicago, and State Championship. The very first tournament that I competed in I took third place. The first world championship was so successful in Chicago that they brought it back to Chicago the next year, and it was held at the Chicago Coliseum. And I took second place at the world championship. I think I had around 13 matches and I won every one of them except the last one. We didn't have what you call a light- or heavy-weight division. There weren't any different rankings. You fought everybody. And Lou Friend, who I had just beat several weeks prior in the Midwest championship ended up beating me. I underestimated Lou. Lou was a man who did not have a lot of feet. And I'd beat him pretty good. And I had good feet. And so I guess he must have practiced a little bit and really surprised me. So that the story behind that is never go in a match thinking about what you have seen that person do before. Fight the man and let the techniques develop and work whatever happens. Don't go in anticipating.

In class we worked basic techniques every day, every one of those blocks, kicks, punches, strikes we worked, including the exercises. But I understood the principles and I was hungry for information. I would read a lot of books and I would look at things and say, `What about this?' I was analyzing and changing and redirecting because I wasn't really satisfied in obtaining my black belt in 13 months. Therefore, I really made it my business to try to learn as much about it as I possibly could, through reading, through talking to people, through mostly thinking about it. I can say, almost every waking moment that I had, I was thinking about martial arts.

From martial arts training I gained confidence. The ability to talk and deal with people. To be able to express my opinion.

My instructor John Keehan was probably one of the best martial arts practitioners I ever saw. Through all the hype, he was one of the best, had

Jones' first instructor, John Keehan...Photo Courtesy of Jones.

some of the best form, was the only man today that I've ever seen able to kick a brick in half with a side kick. Punch it with a forefist strike and break it. The guy had tremendous form and a tremendous love for the art. He was a great promoter, he said I don't care what kind of publicity, good or bad, as long as it's publicity, I'll take it.

Ray Cooper also impressed me. Ray was at the Chicago Judo and Karate Center when I first got there. He was a brown belt when I was a white belt. That tournament that I took first place in the brown, he took second in black. He was fighting a guy named Mike Stone and that's when the first drop kick was used. It was invented by Ray Cooper, better known as Tolo-Naa today.

My first school was the Southtown YMCA in Chicago. I started at Southtown because I wanted to bring the art to people who could not afford it. I know when I first got involved in martial arts my mother thought I was crazy. `Boy, why are you spending $20 a month to kick your legs up in the air. What good is it going to do you?' I had no plans or no aspirations to teach the art. It's just something that I grew to love and wanted to be involved in. And so I wanted to give it to the people who could least afford it. And I thought it was an excellent way of disciplining and developing children. The Y had all the facilities and space that I needed. That's why I didn't have to pay and they split the fee between the Y and myself, therefore nothing came out of my pocket and everybody benefited from it. So I started to teach at Southtown. Southtown grew to one of the top schools in the Chicagoland area.

There were maybe 50 or more students in the class. Matter of fact, when we traveled to tournaments we rented buses and we rented train cars, whole railroad train cars to travel. When we went to Kansas City we had two train cars of people to go down with us. And we won the Grand National down there. We took first place in sparring and second place in Kata. So we got a lot of exposure in the press, in the newspapers and in the media

(beginning second from left) Mfundishi Tolo-Naa, Bob Trias, John Keehan, Mike Stone, Lou Friend, James Jones, Jr.
Photo Courtesy of James Jones, Jr.

when we came back after winning the national championships. We also did a lot of promotions. We did promotions for Matel, G.I. Joe and all the rest of the things. We were very popular because we were a winning school. I also left Southtown once I had students that had developed enough to teach .

Initially no one at that time gave tournaments in the Chicagoland area except John Keehan and then he died. So I started to be the tournament promoter. I had the facilities because the Y was free and at my disposal. And I got the idea why not try to build an organization within the Chicagoland area through the YMCAs. I became in charge of all the YMCAs for Illinois and Indiana and I had all the Karate classes under my control. So, as my students developed I started to place them in the Ys throughout the city. And nobody could give a tournament until I got there. And we did have control, at least I had control at the time, and I tried to talk to my students to tell them and to try to get them to look at things in a very businesslike way, which was very difficult for them. It's hard to have other people live your dream. It actually did work out and then more and more people got involved in tournaments.

I started to teach for Charles Brown who owned the first black commercial martial arts school in Chicago. After really looking at the business, I said why only make a couple hundred dollars a week when I can make thousands of dollars? I said I'm making the money for somebody else. If I'm going to teach I should teach for myself. So that's when I decided to open up my own school commercially. I promised Charles that I would never take any of his students. I wouldn't allow any of his students to come to my school.

So I opened up JJ Karate, Limited in 1972 and the school was an instant success. I had built a reputation. It happened because I had thought through the process of how to open a school. And I think there's an art to opening a school. I gave my first major tournament at McCormick Place in 1972

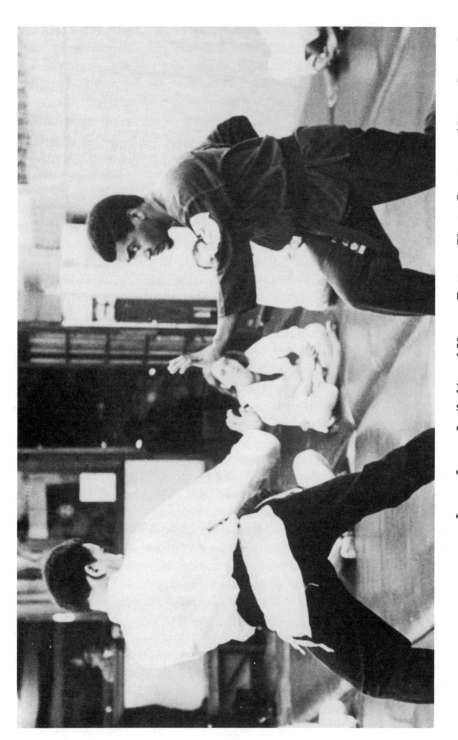

James Jones, Jr. (left) and Kenny Patton...Photo Courtesy of James Jones, Jr.

because I wanted to try to bring the martial arts up to a different level, a national level. So many of us are satisfied with very little. I wasn't that type of individual. I wanted to see it grow. I wanted to make it into something more than what you typically see in a gymnasium. It's HOW you put on a show. I wanted something that looked professional and organized. And so when I put on the show at McCormick Place, I thought we had lifted the martial arts into a new era.

Robert Trias, who was considered one of the founders of Karate in America, had asked me to put together something for the American public in 1974. We had no particular style that we Americans could call our own. As martial artists know, basically a system is designed around the physical characteristics of the people that are in a particular area. Americans have good size and stature. We have good hands, good feet. We have long legs. So why not utilize the best of our body to work with, both hands and feet? I decided to utilize the strength of the different styles such as the Chinese soft style and the Japanese style with the hard, direct attack, speed. I had studied Aikido and I had studied Judo, Karate and a little Ju-jutsu. That's how the Universal system came about. I had studied the Tiger form, the Snake, the Crane, the Dragon, and the Leopard. And that's what the universal consists of, the five major animal forms and the Snake was the main form we worked out of. And that's when we developed the five Hebinos. "Hebino Yatte Kata" Ben Peacock, Tayari Casel, and I mainly put it together.

Because of my attitude about teaching. I've always felt that I wanted to produce teachers of the art. I wanted my people to be able to go any place in this world and be recognized as good martial artists, whether they knew who I was or not. Once they saw my student apply his technique, they would say, `This guy knows what the hell he's doing.'

I designed my dojo differently. I had full mirrors across the wall, so that people could see what they were doing. I got tired of my feet being cold, so I

James Jones Jr. (right) and students...Photo Courtesy of James Jones Jr.

had carpet put down. And I tried to make it look professional. So often schools look like a dirty gym, dirty locker rooms, and dirty everything else. That was something I wasn't raised around and I didn't like it. And I wanted my school to look professional, as professional as I could afford to have it look.

I laid out the classes, what I wanted taught. And my instructors taught from a work book. As long as they worked from this book they couldn't go wrong. There's a trick to that. There's an art to running a class and running a school because of the constant influx of people joining. It's sort of disruptive unless you have procedures and set ways of doing it to bring a student along. Many, many martial arts people don't do that. They just blend that person in. But it's unfair to the student. It's unfair to the other people in the school to do that. I think it's critical that as you develop your students, you develop a philosophy, you develop class participation, you develop teaching experience. I had set it up so that you had to have so many teaching hours in order to move along, which in turn reinforced the learning that the student has gained. You're constantly giving. Everybody has to give back to the people that are coming up. But the school grew well and eventually in 1980 I decided to drop out of the martial arts world.

I looked for myself in my students. I looked for a better person in them from when they come in to when they go out. When they leave me I want to see a better Kata, a better person, a person who can understand and deal with life on a higher plane, not on the same level as when they first came to me. An instructor should have an impact on a student. The student should believe in you as Sensei and it should mean something. It should be just like family. It should be a bond between that instructor and the student.

The most successful student that I have had is Ken Knudson, he was the first Caucasian that I taught. He came to me over at the Southtown YMCA, which was an all-black, rough area. This young white kid in his early teens and twenties came all

James Jones, Jr. (left) and Ted Love...Photo Courtesy of James Jones, Jr.

the way from the far North Side to study under me because he had heard that I was one of the best. And he came every night that we had class for two years. And he worked with some brothers that he knew that would put a hurt on him if he didn't get out there and fight. And he fought well and he was one of the top students that I had.

Tayari Casel, he stayed at my house just like my house was his house. He was there with me from the time he was that tall all the way until he was a man. Ben Peacock was also one of my success stories. Ben is probably one of the best Kata practitioners in the country, weapons or empty hand. John Norman was another top competitor of mine. He was a fierce fighter. Preston Baker, Otis Baker, Al Campbell, Teddy Love were excellent. Deborah Nathan was an excellent female student. Another is Mary Hodge, who is with one of the detective units in the city today. I've produced many black belts that I can be proud of what they have accomplished and achieved out there.

There's a tremendous difference between martial artists of the past and present. I think that we have lost a lot in one respect and gained a lot in another. I think that the techniques are much more fancy and much more exciting today. They have gained in speed and they have greater physical prowess. In the past there wasn't a lot of movement. The basic techniques were what we worked from. Everything was worked out of one of the basic 13 stances. Now everything is worked out of Hachichi or a modified Kiba. I think the downfall really came with the introduction of the safety kick and the safety punch. In the past no one ever got really seriously hurt because you were taught control, Kime, focus. In the past you had to work precision techniques. You might fight 13 people. You had to be good to get through a tournament. You didn't fight one or two fights and consider yourself a champion. And that's what the five degrees of focus of control are supposed to be about. Be able to hit that man where you want to hit him and how you want to hit him and with what amount of strength or force you want to punch.

Preston and Otis Baker sparring...Photo Courtesy of James Jones, Jr.

And I don't think that they do that today. You see a lot of techniques thrown with no balance. You wouldn't even recognize the technique if you saw it. You don't recognize the fundamentals because there are none. It's just street fighting with a few kicks thrown in today.

The mental aspect is missing as well because it's not taught as an art form. It's taught as a method of fighting. The art form takes in the whole thing. That's what makes it an art, the spiritual, the mental aspect, as well as the physical aspect. When we lose any of those, we lose the art. And I think that's what we've done. We don't even work Kata. Most people don't spar, don't work Kata. Why don't they work Kata? Because Kata's a discipline. It makes you work things precisely, a specific way. Half the Katas you see today are modified because it makes it easier.

As far as the mental aspect, forget it. Any black belt can promote a child to black belt or a teenager to black belt. What can a teenager offer other than the physical ability to perform a technique? He can't give back. I think it's a mistake to put that child in that situation.

I would tell anyone seeking martial arts to visit a number of schools. Get a feel for the instructors. Ask them what they're teaching and how they teach. I think a class has to be structured in a way that a person can continue to grow. If there's no structure to the class then it's going to be haphazard. A good instructor has a blueprint for success in how you can move that person along and how you can accomplish goals.

My philosophy on life has changed. I'm not as ambitious as I used to be. It doesn't interest me any more to make a lot of money. It interests me to be successful in the things that I do, in the endeavors that I do. For instance I'm bowling and I shot my first 300 game last year. I golf a lot. I'm trying to get in the 70s, which I just missed the other day by two strokes. But these are things or goals that I'm trying to accomplish. I have two young kids that I like to

UNITED STATES KARATE ASSOCIATION

ARIZONA • ALABAMA • ALASKA • CALIFORNIA • COLORADO • CONNECTICUT
ENGLAND • FLORIDA • GEORGIA • HAWAII • ILLINOIS • INDIANA • IOWA
JAPAN • KANSAS • KOREA • LOUISIANA • MAINE • MASSACHUSETTS • MEXICO
MINNESOTA • MISSOURI • NEBRASKA
NEW JERSEY • NEW YORK • NEW
MEXICO • NEW HAMPSHIRE • NORTH
CAROLINA • OHIO • OKINAWA
OKLAHOMA • OREGON • PENNSYLVANIA
PHILIPPINE IS. • PUERTO RICO • SOUTH
AFRICA • SOUTH DAKOTA • TENNESSEE
TEXAS • UTAH • WEST VIRGINIA
WISCONSIN

CERTIFICATE OF RANK

Karate-ka ___James A. Jones Jr.___ is hereby granted
the rank of ___1st Grade Black Belt___ ___Sho-dan___ with the United States Karate
Association in recognition of the progress, ability and knowledge that has been accomplished by the
diligent study and practice in the Okinawa-Japanese origin art of Karate. It is our wish that the Karate-ka
will endeavor to improve further in the physical, mental and spiritual forces that are involved in the daily
study and practice of this martial art.

望ムモノ也　道ニ精進サレン事ヲ　励ミ心身共ニ此ノ空手　モ猶怠ル事ナク修行ニ　タフニ進級ノ証ヲ与ヘ今後　セル知識顕著也依ツテ　其ノ進歩其ダシク修得　空手道修業ニ精励シ　上記之者日本及ビ沖縄

Per Authority of U.S.K.A.
Director Robert A. Trias____

Date __September 6th__ 19 64   U.S.K.A. No. __228__

_____
8th Dan U.S.A.
6th Dan Okinawa

_____
5th Dan Japan
4th Dan Korea

___John Von Nutton___
USKA Representative

James Jones, Jr.'s first degree black belt certificate...Courtesy of Jones.

see grow and develop.

I've gotten a lot out of the martial arts. I've gotten a great deal of self-satisfaction from something that I enjoyed and loved. To love anything is enjoyable. There's a great deal of satisfaction in loving, even more so, loving, than to be loved. To love something you give all of yourself to it and you enjoy it, every bit of it, the good and the bad. That's how I feel about martial arts. I got a great deal of love from it, excitement, and travel. It opened up a lot of doors for me. It has helped me on my job today. The reason that I'm in the position that I'm in today is because the chairman of the company came to every show I ever had. Here's a man who's got millions and millions of dollars, but he would take time, he would come to all my shows and talk to me. And he knew that I had good business sense. I didn't go to the colleges. I was more of a self-made man. So he saw this in me. He knew that I could deal with people. So he took me out of the shop and put me in charge of all the hiring for his company. I went from a lowly sweeper to the gardener, to the mechanic, to the maintenance man, to the assistant supervisor, to the superintendent, to the manager of the personnel department. It's just a matter of how you look at things and what you want to achieve.

I think I gave a great deal. I gave the Kata forms that I developed. I gave back teachers. I gave a great deal of love and my life. I think I set trends when I was there, when I was active. I gave the biggest shows in this area of the country. I tried to be a good representative for the exposure that I had with the public. I hope the world, our society, are better off because of the people I trained. I have students who became accountants. I have students that are lawyers. I have students that are in television and in the movies. And I've always said to all of my students, `I want you to be better than me. If you do that, I'm happy. I'm satisfied.' I think so many of us have that fear of fading into the sunset. We're going to all do that. Ashes to ashes and dust to dust. It's not what we do. It's what we leave behind. And that lasts forever because it perpetu-

James Jones, Jr. (middle, back row) at New York vs. Chicago tournament...Photo Courtesy of James Jones, Jr.

ates itself and others carry it forth. If they carry on your spirit and the thoughts and the things that you've done when you were here, then you're still here.

Preston Baker, James Jones, Jr., K. Vita, Bob Bowles (left to right).
Photo Courtesy of James Jones, Jr.

William F. Hinton

About the Authors

William F. Hinton started his martial arts training
at the age of seventeen in the art of Karate. Hinton
is an active member of both the AAU (Amateur
Athletic Union) and the USAKF (United States
Karate Federation). Hinton has represented both
organizations as a national and international competitor, as well as functioning as a coach and official. Hinton continues to teach Karate in addition
to giving motivational lectures to college and high
school students on the benefits of self-discipline.
Hinton received his B.A. from Northeastern Illinois
University in Sociology and Criminal Justice; he
received two M.A.s from the University of Chicago:
the first in East Asian Languages and Civilizations,
specializing in Japanese History; the second, in
Urban Studies, specializing in Urban Economic
Development.

D'Arcy J. Rahming

About the Authors

D'Arcy J. Rahming's martial arts credentials include black belts in Karate, Judo, and Ju-jutsu. He is the author and producer of the Combat Ju-jutsu book and video series, as well as The College Student's Complete Guide to Self-Protection. Rahming has served as a consultant to police and federal agencies on designing use-of-force courses. He received his B.S. in electrical engineering and his M.B.A. in finance from Northwestern University. Rahming continues to teach the traditional martial arts of Karate, Judo and Ju-jutsu and self-protection seminars to college students and community groups.

Index

A

Aikido 19, 20, 58, 60, 62, 63, 71, 72, 74, 76, 78, 80, 82, 132

B

Brown, Robert 59, 71, 98, 102

C

Cheatham, James (Chea Chea) 47, 48, 51, 53, 54, 56, 85, 86, 90, 91, 97, 102

Cooper, Raymond 60, 64, 66, 94, 97, 128

D

Dojo 14, 38, 45, 48, 52, 53, 72, 91, 98, 100, 104, 114, 115, 116, 120, 132

Duncan, Ronald 35

F

Field, James 113

H

Harris, George 19, 44

J

James, Gilbert 71

Japan Karate Association (JKA) 13, 113, 114, 115,

122, 123

Jones, James (Jimmie) 13, 14, 60, 98, 125

Judo 7, 8, 13, 19, 20, 24, 25, 26, 30, 33, 35, 36, 44, 47, 48, 59, 62, 71, 72, 78, 82, 85, 97, 125, 128, 132

Ju-jutsu 7, 8, 12, 19, 20, 35, 44, 59, 71, 72, 82, 85, 132

K

Karate 7, 8, 10, 12, 13, 14, 19, 20, 28, 35, 47, 48, 50, 54, 59, 60, 62, 63, 64, 66, 71, 72, 75, 78, 82, 85, 86, 87, 91, 97, 98, 99, 100, 102, 113, 114, 115, 118, 120, 122, 125, 128, 130, 132

Kobu-jutsu 71, 72, 82

Kung Fu 13, 100

L

LaPuppet, Thomas 38

M

Maasi, Shaha Mfundishi 38, 47, 85

Moseley, Louis 7

N

Nichols, William 38, 47, 85

P

Powell, Moses 38

R

Racism 5, 99, 100

EXPLOSIVE SECRETS OF SELF-PROTECTION
The best books and videos on self-protection available !!

Secrets of Miyama Ryu Combat
Combat Ju-jutsu - The Lost Art
by D'Arcy Rahming $18.95

Stop an attacker in his tracks with Combat Ju-jutsu. This is the grandfather of the Japanese martial arts. It includes the power-packed strikes of Karate, the awesome throws of Judo and the crushing joint-locks of Aikido, ONLY BETTER! ! Now the secrets of Ju-jutsu have been updated for the streets of America. This easy to use guide takes you step-by-step through each movement. You'll feel as if there is an instructor standing right beside you.

Secrets of Advanced Combat Ju-jutsu
by D'Arcy Rahming $24.95

Walk without fear. This title includes over 200 devastating techniques to prepare you for your black belt. Ju-jutsu is considered one of the most effective forms of self-defense available today. This classic text is for you. **Secrets** details the Miyama Ryu Ju-jutsu system in over 900 illustrations and 228 pages or in our 50 minute VHS video. **Secrets** picks up where Combat Ju-jutsu left off. Order it today and you'll learn how to make 400 years of tradition work for you.

Men of Steel Discipline
The Official Oral History of Black Pioneers in the
Martial Arts by William Hinton $19.95

Revealed at last! These are the untold true stories of ten pioneers who influenced the course of martial arts in America. **Men of Steel Discipline** is an inspirational guide and a must for every serious martial artist. If you thought you knew everything about the early days of martial arts in America, these never before published stories will shock you. Over 150 pages including 47 rare, historical, action photos.